NOLO *Your Legal Companion*

"In Nolo you can trust." —**THE NEW YORK TIMES**

Whether you have a simple question or a complex problem, turn to us at:

NOLO.COM

Your all-in-one legal resource

Need quick information about wills, patents, adoptions, starting a business—or anything else that's affected by the law? **Nolo.com** is packed with free articles, legal updates, resources and a complete catalog of our books and software.

NOLO NOW

Make your legal documents online

Creating a legal document has never been easier or more cost-effective! Featuring Nolo's Online Will, as well as online forms for LLC formation, incorporation, divorce, name change—and many more! Check it out at **http://nolonow.nolo.com**.

NOLO'S LAWYER DIRECTORY

Meet your new attorney

If you want advice from a qualified attorney, turn to Nolo's Lawyer Directory—the only directory that lets you see hundreds of in-depth attorney profiles so you can pick the one that's right for you. Find it at **http://lawyers.nolo.com**.

ALWAYS UP TO DATE

Sign up for NOLO'S LEGAL UPDATER

Old law is bad law. We'll email you when we publish an updated edition of this book—sign up for this free service at nolo.com/legalupdater.

Find the latest updates at NOLO.COM

Recognizing that the law can change even before you use this book, we post legal updates during the life of this edition at **nolo.com/updates**.

Is this edition the newest? ASK US!

To make sure that this is the most recent available, just give us a call at **800-728-3555**.

(Please note that we cannot offer legal advice.)

1st edition

Small Business in Paradise

Working for Yourself in a Place You Love

by Michael Molinski

FIRST EDITION	OCTOBER 2007
Editor	TAMARA TRAEDER
Cover Design	SUSAN WIGHT
Book Design	SUSAN PUTNEY
Proofreading	ROBERT WELLS
Index	BAYSIDE INDEXING SERVICE
Printing	CONSOLIDATED PRINTERS, INC.

Molinski, Michael, 1963-
    Small business in paradise : working for yourself in a place you love / by Michael Molinski. -- 1st ed.
        p. cm.
    Includes index.
    ISBN-13: 978-1-4133-0743-6 (pbk.)
    ISBN-10: 1-4133-0743-4 (pbk.)
    1. New business enterprises. 2. Small business--Management. 3. Entrepreneurship. I
Title.
HD62.5.M637 2007
658.02'2--dc22
                        2007018487

Quantity sales: For information on bulk purchases or corporate premium sales, please contact the Special Sales Department. For academic sales or textbook adoptions, ask for Academic Sales. Call 800-955-4775 or write to Nolo, 950 Parker Street, Berkeley, CA 94710.

Acknowledgments

First and foremost, I'd like to thank all of the small business owners who took the time to tell me their stories and impart such valuable advice. Their entrepreneurship and passion for what they do are models for us all. And a special thanks to Jan Peterson of Jan's Mountain Outfitters, who helped plant the seeds for this book.

A huge thank you to all the people at Nolo, especially my editor, Tamara Traeder, whose contributions to the book went well beyond editing. A special thank you also to Nolo editorial staff Marcia Stewart and Lexi Elmore, who contributed much valuable material and helped with final edits; Janet Portman, for her time and expertise on the subject of leasing business space; and Lisa Guerin, who provided valuable insight on hiring employees and other help. Thank you also to the other Nolo authors and editors who shared their expertise; to Nolo's creative production staff (especially Susan Wight who came up with such a wonderful cover and Susan Putney who designed this book); and to all of those in Nolo publicity, marketing, and sales, for their hard work and genuine interest in the book's success.

And finally, thank you to my sons, Nick and Nathan, for their patience (Yes, we did finish the tree house before the book!), and to Jairun Nisha, my partner in paradise, for her inspiration and unwavering support.

Table of Contents

The Dream's Not Always the Same

You've been working in the same field for 20 or 30 years.

The rat race is getting to you.

You're bored, tired, burned out.

You're looking for a change.

You start to wonder what else is out there.

Sound familiar? Millions of Americans find themselves in the same predicament. And at one time or another, many of them (you perhaps?) consider moving to some remote locale, living simply, and starting a business. The dream business, however, isn't always the same. It may be a bar in Key West, a surf shop in Costa Rica, a winery in Napa, or a ski shop in Aspen, among many other possibilities. Perhaps it's not a new business that populates the dream, but a new locale—you visualize your accounting firm in Vermont, your restaurant in Maui, your dental office on Bainbridge Island, or your consulting firm just about anywhere. Regardless, the dream may remain just that—a dream. For whatever reason, whether lacking funding, know-how, or just plain old energy, your plans may not have gotten off the ground. You stay in your job, and count the years to retirement.

If you are feeling dissatisfied, you are certainly not alone. Consider that a whopping three-fourths of U.S. workers are either actively or passively looking for a new job at any given time, according to the 2006 U.S. Job Retention Survey, conducted by the Society for Human Resource Management (SHRM). For those who voluntarily left their jobs in 2006, the motivating factor was often less about money or career opportunities, and increasingly about the need for a change. "Ready for a new experience" was the second biggest reason that employees left their jobs in 2006, according to the survey. That reason moved up from a distant fourth place just two years earlier. Similarly, "Career change" also moved up sharply, to fifth place in 2006 from eighth place in 2004.

Those statistics suggest that Americans, or at least a good percentage of them, are becoming increasingly tired of the rat race. They are deriving less and less satisfaction from working in corporate America, feeling bored and underappreciated, fed up with an increasing lack of job security and the perception of poor management. They are also finding it harder and harder to balance work and life issues, according to the SHRM survey.

Some U.S. companies are getting the hint, and are initiating new programs specifically designed to retain valuable employees—merit bonuses, career development opportunities, flexible work schedules and telecommuting, child care, and more vacation time. For instance, American Express encourages workers to switch jobs within the company after 12 to 24 months, so they don't get burned out. Timberland pays employees to work up to 40 hours at volunteer jobs outside the company. Genentech, like many other companies, rewards employees by making them shareholders—95% of Genentech employees own shares in the company. Still, they have been unable to stop the flow. Increasingly, Americans are striking out on their own—setting up small businesses or sole proprietorships, becoming contractors, working from home. The number of independent contractors in the U.S. grew to 10.3 million, or 7.4% of the total employed workforce in 2005, and up from 6.4% in 2001, according to the U.S. Department of Labor. Meanwhile, temporary workers have also been steadily climbing, to 1.8% of the workforce in 2005 from 1.1% in 1990.

Daniel Pink, author of *Free Agent Nation*, points out that fewer than one in ten Americans now work for a Fortune 500 Company, and that the largest private employer in America, by body count, is no longer General Motors, AT&T, or even Microsoft—it's Manpower, Inc., the temporary employment agency. According to Pink, an increasing number of Manpower's workers are choosing temporary work because it offers a better work-life balance, not because they cannot find permanent work.

More and more entrepreneurs are setting up shop—not in the big metropolitan areas where they have been pursuing their livelihoods, but in paradise—the resort towns, mountain communities, island retreats, and beaches of the world—where keeping up with the Joneses gives way to pursuing a certain quality of life. For example, the number of wineries now tops 5,000, up from less than 3,000 in 2000, and the number of bed and breakfasts now numbers over 20,000, up from just 1,000 in 1980.

Meanwhile, another major trend—the aging of America—is contributing to the increased focus on living in paradise. There are 78 million baby boomers in America, and they started hitting retirement age in 2006. However, many of them are not even considering "retirement" in the traditional sense of the word. The number of Americans aged 65 or older who have remained, or plan to remain, in the work force is rising, from 10% in 1985 to 13% in 2002, and a projected 16%, or 26.6 million workers, in 2010, according to the U.S. Department of the Census and the AARP Foundation.

While many of those workers will continue doing the same type of work they have always done (except perhaps less of it and on their own terms), many others are looking for a change, both in career and lifestyle. For many of those individuals, a small business in paradise is the perfect solution—offering recent retirees the career change and active involvement they seek, while also providing a quality of life they always dreamed retirement could offer.

A Road Map to Turning Your Dream Into Reality

This book is about turning a dream into reality. But not so fast—running a small business in paradise isn't always, well, paradise! As with any other worthy goal, launching a business successfully takes careful planning and meticulous execution. Further, it may take years before the start-up headaches are over and you finally hit the comfort zone of operating an established, successful business. Despite the challenges, many have succeeded in creating their businesses in paradise. Is it for you?

Reading the next 13 chapters may help you discover the answer. As a quick preview, Chapters 2 through 5 focus on personal stories of individuals and couples who have taken the plunge into paradise, including:

- entrepreneurs in particular industries (bed and breakfasts and wineries)
- individuals who became business owners (of a candy store, a Caribbean bar, and a marketing consulting firm) somewhat unexpectedly, either being offered an opportunity or creating a business in response to life's circumstances, and
- people who have transformed their passions into businesses, including a restaurateur, a gallery owner, a photographer, and a surfer.

In addition to recounting the real-life experiences of these business owners, these chapters provide insights on how they've managed to overcome obstacles, build successful small businesses, and integrate those businesses into their lives and livelihoods. After sharing in these entrepreneurs' experiences, the rest of the book delves deeper into the various aspects of setting up a small business, and factors to consider that make businesses in resort or tourist destinations different from others. These include:

- a ten-step plan for getting started with your business in paradise, including making sure the business is a good fit with you and your loved ones, learning more about the business and locale you are considering, putting together a business plan and financing, and creating a backup plan (Chapter 6)
- issues to consider when choosing a business location and negotiating a lease (Chapter 7)
- ways to make the most of the seasonal ups and downs that paradise businesses usually experience (Chapter 8)

- tips on working with both a seasonal and a year-round workforce (Chapter 9)
- how to develop a marketing plan with an emphasis on community involvement, the key to getting your business established in a small community (Chapters 10 and 11),
- an introduction to the tax and legal issues you'll likely consider in setting up your business (Chapter 12), and
- how to make starting a business a component of a responsible financial plan, as well as enhancing your lifestyle (Chapter 13).

Throughout, you'll read more stories of other entrepreneurs who have pursued their dream, and gain practical guidance about what worked for them. As you see what others have done, perhaps you will feel more confident that your dream could be your reality, and be inspired to get started.

The Bed and Breakfast Biz

S urely the bed and breakfast (B&B) is one of the businesses most dreamed about by those looking for an escape to paradise. There are some 20,000 B&Bs in North America, approximately 87% of them in tourist and resort destinations. Most of them are run by couples, often romantically involved but sometimes just business partners. Many are baby boomers who left the corporate world for a new start—and a career in paradise.

What's a B&B, Exactly?

PAII defines a B&B as a lodging establishment that also serves as residence for the owner-hosts and serves a breakfast meal to its overnight guests. B&Bs also include "country inns" which serve dinner to their visitors in addition to breakfast.

According to the Professional Association of Innkeepers International (PAII), growth in the B&B industry rocketed up in the 1980s and 1990s and has continued climbing, albeit at a slower pace, over the last several years, with $3.4 billion in revenue in 2006, up from $3.1 billion in 2002. That growth is attributable to several factors: On the demand side, weekend travelers are getting away from the typical motel or hotel stays and looking for something more off-the-beaten-track. Plus, growth in the overall economy has fueled tourism, and the difficulties in air travel since the attacks of September 11, 2001 have prompted more people to get in their car. Car travel favors B&Bs because they tend to be far from major airports but often within a few hours drive of the major cities where their guests reside. On the supply side, the number of B&Bs has continued to grow (there were only about 1,000 nationwide in 1980), although that growth has slowed considerably since the 1990s. Still, occupancy rates have gone up—to an average of 43% in 2006 from 38% in 2002—and B&Bs have become much more efficient in the way they do business.

FIND OUT MORE

The Professional Association of Innkeepers International website (www.paii.org) is an excellent source for aspiring innkeepers. Among other useful information, the website maintains a list of upcoming seminars and workshops on running B&Bs, a list of reading resources and best practices in the B&B industry, state associations, and lots more. This leading B&B association will send you a free guide for aspiring innkeepers, if you send them an email.

There has also been a dramatic shift in the nature of B&B ownership: "Twenty years ago, many people who were interested in starting B&Bs just wanted to save these great old historic homes, and live in them. Now, most of the old homes have been saved and the people who are buying B&Bs aren't as motivated by historic preservation," says Pam Horovitz, president of PAII. Today, lifestyle constitutes the biggest component of the purchase decision. And increasingly, B&B ownership is becoming a business choice: People are deciding to open B&Bs because it can be an enjoyable and profitable business venture. Consequently, B&Bs have sprouted up wherever there is a demand for them, regardless of whether an old mansion or simple farmhouse is available.

Is a B&B Suited to You?

Owning and running a B&B is not for everyone. The turnover rate for B&B ownership ranges from 15% to 20% per year, reflecting the fact that many innkeepers discover the reality of running one is not what they had envisioned. A national survey of B&B owners conducted by PAII found only 42% had owned their respective B&Bs for seven years or more, while 24% had maintained ownership for four to six years, and 34% for three years or less.

If you are aspiring to be a B&B owner, PAII poses three key questions to help you determine whether that business is a good fit for you:

- **How much do you like people?** If you value seclusion, owning a B&B is not for you. You must feel comfortable opening up your home to a constant stream of strangers, and enjoy their visits and your interaction with them.

- **Do you enjoy serving people?** Innkeeping is first and foremost a service business. Your job will include providing an aesthetically pleasing, quiet, clean bed and breakfast, but also waiting on guests, listening to their stories, answering their questions, and making restaurant reservations for them—and doing it all with a smile.

- **Do you like being your own boss?** A B&B is a business like any other, and owning a business carries certain risks and responsibilities that working for others does not. However, the control you have over your decisions and how you spend your day can make those responsibilities seem worth it, just as it has for thousands of B&B owners.

Still interested? Then read on.

Love, Work, and a B&B

If there is one region where B&Bs particularly flourish, it is New England. From Maine to Connecticut, Massachusetts to Vermont, the New England landscape is littered with these businesses. The B&B high season typically runs from mid-May through early November in New England (but of course varies widely for other parts of the country).

Cape Cod is perhaps the center of New England's B&B heaven. This small sliver of land just east of Boston has been home over the centuries to some of this country's most famous—and infamous—personalities. From the Pilgrims of nearby Plymouth, to the Kennedys of Hyannis Port, Cape Cod's history incorporates much of the American experience. It is also home to some of the most exquisitely elegant historic mansions found anywhere on the planet—and the perfect spot for the roughly 250 active bed and breakfasts that populate it.

What you won't see when you tour this charming and historic region, however, are the multitudes of B&Bs that have gone out of business. Cape Cod has one of the nation's highest turnover rates for B&B owners, and some of the strictest regulations governing B&B ownership. Many of the B&Bs that have failed here have done so because of the sharp rise in property prices. Like other popular B&B regions—Santa Barbara, California, and Park City, Utah, for example—Cape Cod B&B owners have been caught in a real estate bubble that has driven up the cost of maintaining a B&B. As a result, many area B&Bs have reverted to being private homes.

As daunting as that sounds, some people have achieved success in the B&B business on Cape Cod—even after a relatively recent start and during a period of rapidly escalating property prices. For instance, two couples—Vince Toreno and Patricia Martin, and Cecily Denson and Richard Pratt have, rather recently, made the jump to B&B ownership on Cape Cod. It's obvious from both couples' experiences that buying and running a B&B takes moxie, patience, and a strong sense of commitment—both to the business and to each other.

The first couple, Vince Toreno and Patricia Martin, were the king and queen of business travel. Both worked at Polaroid—Vince as national sales manager, Patricia as international marketing director. They met some years earlier at a trade show in New Orleans.

In his sales career, Vince spent his life traveling to sales meetings and trade shows—always with briefcase in hand and suit bag slung over his shoulder, and almost always staying at big-city chain hotels where the companies he worked for enjoyed corporate rates. "I was from South Florida (home of many luxury, big-chain resorts), and, when it came to staying in hotels, I was a Marriot kind of guy," Vince recalls. Patricia, on the other hand, preferred to stay at smaller inns and B&Bs when she traveled. As the international marketing director for Polaroid, Patricia's travels often took her to Europe, introducing her to a European style of innkeeping that she later incorporated into her B&B management on Cape Cod.

Before dating Patricia, Vince had never spent a night in a B&B. During their courtship, she introduced him to a life touring New England, where they shopped for antiques and—you guessed it—stayed at B&Bs. "The first one we went to had a common bath. What an experience!" Vince remembers. Nevertheless, he was surprised how his initial hesitancy turned into almost an overnight appreciation for the charm of B&B lodgings.

Vince and Patricia later married. Patricia's love of antiques and B&Bs became Vince's love too—something they shared as a couple. They bought a home and settled into life in Belmont, Massachusetts, a suburb of Boston.

In 1999, Polaroid began to have serious financial troubles as newer digital technologies surpassed its aging "instamatic" cameras. The livelihood that had been Patricia's security blanket for 20 years began to erode, and at 49, Patricia was still six years away from the minimum retirement age. "I didn't think the company would last long enough for me to hit retirement. Besides, the job was changing. I just realized I was no longer going to have the same opportunities and a budget to continue to do the things I was doing. So, when I got offered a severance program, I took it." Sure enough, Polaroid went into bankruptcy protection in 2001 and the company's assets were sold.

After leaving Polaroid, Patricia decided to try to make a career out of her antiques hobby. She took a class on how to write a business plan, and started building an antiques business. Two years later, Vince retired and began working part time as a sales consultant, still traveling with Patricia throughout New England to hunt down antiques for her business.

"We were doing well but not well enough," Patricia remembers of the antiques business. The more they traveled, the more the idea of opening their own B&B took hold. "There was just something over the years that appealed to us about B&Bs. We loved the idea of having a historic home. And as we were collecting antiques I needed a place to display them and use them to entertain. You couldn't do that every day at home, but you could in a B&B. It just seemed to fit."

Prior to conducting their search, Vince and Patricia had put together a "must-have" list and a "nice-to-have" list to guide their purchase decision. (See Chapter 7 for more about selecting properties for your small business in paradise.) They knew they needed a place that would function well as a B&B, but also be a home in which they would enjoy living. The couple considered Vermont as the locale for their inn, but ruled it out for being too cold. Then, one weekend while visiting friends on the Cape, they started to look around for properties. They quickly realized that many of the desirable B&B properties in the area were all being sold by the same realtor, Jack McDermott. As it turned out, small inns and B&Bs were his specialty—and still is. (A look at McDermott's website, www.capecodinnsforsale.com, in early 2007 showed six B&Bs for sale, ranging in price from $550,000 to $2.5 million—but all of them with a "sold" sign across the announcement.)

A SMALL BUSINESS IN Paradise

If you would like to learn more about Ashley Manor, visit www.ashleymanor.net.

It took Vince and Patricia nine months to find the B&B they wanted. They initially made an offer on another one, but the owner would not wait for the sale of their home in Belmont, so they kept looking. Then their house sold, and the new owners wanted to move into it within four weeks. The B&B Vince and Patricia had initially offered to buy was still available, but before bringing that deal back to life, McDermott took them to see another property, the 300-year-old Ashley Manor in the Cape Cod town of Barnstable.

"We saw it and fell in love instantly," Patricia says. "We knew that if we were going to try the B&B business, it would be in this house. The Ashley Manor was spacious, with high ceilings, big bedrooms, fireplaces, and Jacuzzi tubs in some of the bathrooms. Plus, it was situated on two acres of land in a historic district. It had so much going for it."

The Ashley Manor, however, was not yet for sale. It was early spring, and the owner didn't want to leave for another six months, at the end of the lucrative Cape Cod high season. She eventually agreed to sell after McDermott pointed out that ready buyers such as Vince and Patricia could take months to find, and that they could not wait—their house was already sold and they needed a place to live. Getting the owner's agreement was just the first step in purchasing the property, however. Vince and Patricia then needed to line up financing and also obtain a permit to operate the B&B under local zoning laws. (Unlike many other regions, where a permit to operate an existing B&B would transfer to new owners with the sale of the property, local zoning laws in Cape Cod required an entirely new permit be issued. For more about obtaining approvals of various governmental agencies, see "Registrations, Licenses, and Permits" in Chapter 12.) The permit process required them to appear before the Cape Cod planning commission, and the earliest hearing date was in August. So they waited, and once the planning commission approved their application, they secured a mortgage and bought the Ashley Manor for $1.25 million that same month.

Vince's and Patricia's experience in choosing their inn is typical of Cape Cod B&B owners. Finding the right property usually does not result from combing the real estate listings—many of the best ones are sold before they ever hit the listing stage, either through word of mouth or by real estate professionals like McDermott who have buyers at the ready. A good way to determine what is available is to stay at B&Bs and talk to the owners. Like Vince and Patricia, many of them belong to innkeepers' associations, and they may know of other innkeepers who are considering selling their properties. Prices also vary widely from region to region. The $1.25 million price tag on the Ashley Manor might seem outrageous to someone buying a B&B in parts of the rural South or Midwest, but to Vince and Patricia it was actually quite reasonable. The price of a B&B depends not only on the quality of the property, but also on the level of revenue it produces—a B&B with high occupancy rates in a well-known destination will fetch a higher price. Even in more obscure locations where housing prices are lower, a well-marketed B&B with a steady base of return clients can command a higher price than if its value were based on the property alone.

FIND OUT MORE

In addition to McDermott's website, individuals interested in purchasing a B&B should check out www.bedandbreakfast.com for insight into the market for B&B sales. This comprehensive worldwide listing of B&Bs includes inns for sale, a monthly newsletter, and more.

While Vince and Patricia were happy with their purchase, they immediately realized that the timing of it was a mistake. August is the start of the peak season for Cape Cod B&Bs, and taking ownership that month gave them no time to learn the dos and don'ts of innkeeping. "We were thrown right into the deep end of the pool," Vince recalls.

They survived their trial by fire, but both say that their biggest challenge was making the shift from "married couple" to "business partners who are also married." Couples going into business together often do not realize just how dramatic a change that can be, as Vince describes: "You are business people and you are husband and wife, and sometimes those two conflict with each other." This may be especially true in a business where so many domestic tasks are involved. The division of labor at home that two people may have negotiated over time may no longer work when "home" becomes a B&B, with several roomfuls of guests each night.

Partners in Every Way

According to PAII, 82% of owners of B&Bs are couples.

Vince and Patricia recall waking up on a Sunday morning with a house full of guests, and realizing that neither of them had turned on the dishwasher the night before. Vince would look at her. She would look at him. Tension would rise. "Just making a bed with your partner can be a challenge," Patricia notes.

"It took us a while, but we have managed to define our roles and our responsibilities," Vince says. "And we don't infringe on the other's area. Pat is artistic and methodical. She decorates the rooms. She did the website. She has the marketing background. I am a sales guy. I am in charge of guest relations and long-term strategy. I am also the cook—the kitchen is my domain."

Patricia adds that she is the one who manages the housekeeping and most of the repairs on the home. "I love the handyman stuff." Vince is also responsible for the lawn care and food shopping. They share management of the financial side of the business.

 FIND OUT MORE

Various online sources will provide personal accounts of starting a B&B, and may help you find out if you are interested. The website www.about.com offers a large selection of articles for aspiring B&B owners, many of them with first-person stories about starting and running a successful bed and breakfast. Their articles cover a myriad of related topics as well, from writing a business plan to making sure that the beds don't sag: http://bandb.about.com/cs/aspiring/a/?once=true&.

After three years in business, Vince and Patricia are finally used to the innkeeping routine. They are loving it, and Ashley Manor is thriving. In 2006, they brought in about $175,000 in total revenue, up about

22% from the previous year. Occupancy was up 15%. In the first five months of 2007, they were doing even better—sales of $120,000 were approximately 33% higher than the same period in 2006. They're also starting to diversify their revenue stream. Whereas 2005 revenue comprised almost entirely room rentals, in 2007 about approximately 5% of sales was coming from other activities such as wine and cheese events and the commissions on outsourced spa services and whale watching vouchers.

Profitability, however, is another story. Like many B&B owners, Vince and Patricia plow most of what they make back into property improvements. "We replaced the roof, remodeled two bathrooms, resurfaced the tennis court, replaced furnaces and hot water heaters. We have 75 windows in this house, and we could replace all of them if we wanted to," Vince says. "If we earned a million dollars a year, we would still have things to spend it on."

Why all the spending? The property must be maintained at a certain level to keep their guests coming back and preserve the value of the property. Repairs are also a tax-deductible business expense, so keeping up the property can reduce the business's tax liability. Additionally, most improvements that are not deductible as repair costs may increase the tax basis of the property, but even more importantly, increase its value. Vince sees most of the profit from the business coming from the eventual sale of the property: "You make your money later on, when you sell the place. The reality of this type of business is that with only six guest rooms, our hope is to break even every year. But the business supports our living here—and it truly is a beautiful place to live."

Patricia and Vince have also come to enjoy other aspects of B&B ownership, especially getting to know the interesting people that stay at Ashley Manor. The decrease of the value of the dollar in 2007 in relation to European and British currency has led to an increase in European visitors. They described a recent weekend, during which "we hosted an ex-prima ballerina from the London ballet, the head of a marketing company, and a sports fisherman."

What's next for Vince and Patricia? Their original plan was to keep the place for three to five years, but those plans are evolving. "We're thinking of staying five to seven years now," Vince says. "After that, who knows? We've thought about moving to Napa or Sonoma and opening a winery. With a bed and breakfast, if nobody shows up I can eat the breakfast and sleep in the room. But in a winery, I can drink the wine. And that has an appeal for me!" (Vince should read Chapter 3 for more about opening a winery.)

Buy It, Build It, Flip It

Different individuals derive enjoyment out of different aspects of the B&B industry. Some are attracted to the history of a particular property, and are gratified by their role in preserving that history. Others prefer the hosting role, happily serving, cooking, and entertaining their guests, while still others take pleasure in the design and maintenance aspects of managing a property.

Ten miles up the Cape from Barnstable, in the town of Sandwich, Cecily Denson and Richard Pratt are involved in the industry in a different way—they bought a B&B, restored it, then sold it and bought another (with plans to sell it in the future). Referred to as "flipping" in the real estate industry, the couple has done more than that with their first property—not only did they purchase a property and remodel it, they recharged the B&B business associated with the property.

Like Patricia and Vince, Cecily and Richard came from city life in Boston. She was executive director of the Department of Medicine at Brigham & Women's Hospital before leaving to run her own consulting practice in medical administration. He was a medical researcher at Harvard Medical School. "I had been doing the same thing for almost 30 years. I was tired, burnt out. It was just time for a change," says Richard.

Neither of them had spent much time in B&Bs, and had no particular affinity for them. "I knew I liked running my own shop," recalls Cecily. "We wanted to start a business of our own, and it had to be something we could do together. We looked at all kinds of different things. It could have been a dry cleaning business or a 7-11. But we came across a B&B for sale and I thought, 'Oh, I could do that.'"

They bought the historic Isaiah Jones Homestead in May 2004, for $975,000. It was already operating as an inn with its own clientele, but like most B&Bs, it was decorated in a casual, country floral style. While that style is what most people envision when considering spending a weekend at a B&B, it differentiates little from the competition. Cecily and Richard wanted to change the inn's image, so they restored the property to a Victorian style consistent with the era when it was

A SMALL BUSINESS IN Paradise

If you would like to learn more about the Isaiah Jones Homestead, visit www.isaiahjones.com.

built, decorating it with period antiques and reproductions. The result was a more posh establishment than most of the area B&Bs.

After restoring the inn, Cecily and Richard hoped to attract an upscale clientele who would appreciate—and could afford—the environment they had created. They realized that marketing was essential. "One of the first things we needed to do was spread the word that there was an inn here, and that it was not your typical country-style inn. We wanted our marketing to project something of a classy image," Richard says.

Horovitz of PAII agrees with Richard's strategy: "The best way to increase your occupancy rates is to spend more on marketing. Our recent studies show that the overwhelming majority of B&B owners were planning to significantly increase their expenditures on marketing—particularly online marketing." (To read about other essential components of a small business's marketing plan, see Chapters 10 and 11.)

Tips on Online Marketing

Richard and Cecily shared some of their experiences and advice about marketing their B&B online. They stressed that while Web placements are a key component of a B&B marketing strategy, it is important to do your research before committing money and time to online listings. Some B&B listings cost money, others do not.

- **Paid website listings.** Pick those that are most likely to generate the most business for each dollar you spend on the listing. Ask for the number of unique visitors to each site per month, and also ask other B&B owners in your area which sites they have found useful. Key to your choice of sites is the placement of a particular website in a search engine—i.e., is that site one of the first listed when someone conducts a search on Yahoo! or Google? For example, Richard and Cecily typed in the words "bed & breakfast, cape cod" (without the quotation marks) on Google and found that many of the top listings were on bedandbreakfast.com or on a local site, virtualcapecod.com. So they paid to have their B&B listed on both of those sites. Each placement has brought in numerous clients, far outweighing the cost of placing the listings.

- **Free website listings.** There are also numerous free sites on which B&Bs can be listed, ranging from national bed and breakfast directories to tourism sites, smaller search engines, and local directories. For example, Richard lists their B&B on the lodging sections of local whale-watching sites. It's important to periodically check out the free ones, however, to make sure each site is reputable and does not tarnish your business's image by association.

- **Listings management.** Whether paid or free, keep a running list of all the sites on which your B&B is listed, making sure to update all of them whenever there's a change in your business—especially in pricing information. "If you don't update your prices, clients will find those prices and bring them to your attention, and you end up having to honor them," says Richard.

After three years of managing the inn and building a solid list of clients, Cecily and Richard sold the inn in May 2007 for a price over $1.3 million. They immediately bought another one nearby—the 1830 Quince Tree House, a smaller B&B that is more manageable than the first one, yet more in need of restoration. They'll follow the same process with the Quince Tree House—first envisioning how to differentiate it from other area B&Bs, creating an appealing environment consistent with that vision, building a client base, and then selling it.

Like Vince and Patricia, Richard and Cecily say it's important to understand that running a B&B isn't going to make you a millionaire. "It is very tiring work," Richard says. "You know you've worked a hard summer by the end of the season."

Despite the challenges, Richard and Cecily have found that they enjoy the business of building a B&B as much as running one, and "flipping" seems to afford them a better living in the B&B business. Like Patricia and Vince, they have defined their roles in the day-to-day

A SMALL BUSINESS IN Paradise

If you would like to learn more about 1830 Quince Tree House, visit www.1830quincetreehouse.com.

management: Cecily cooks the breakfasts, and Richard serves them. Richard handles the marketing and business development and most of the major remodeling; Cecily manages the finances, decorating, and housekeeping. But it's the renovation of a new B&B that brings them the most pleasure. And, given that the Isaiah Jones Homestead sold for several hundred thousand dollars more than they paid for it just three years earlier (not including the significant cost of remodeling), it's a pretty good business venture, too.

Richard realizes that profitably flipping B&B properties is dependent on a rising real estate market: "The property we were in was perfect," Richard says of the Isaiah Jones Homestead. "But it was time to do it again. It's not a bad plan as long as the real estate market stays healthy." If the real estate market is slow or in a downturn, however, Richard and

Cecily have the option of hanging on and running the B&B as their livelihood—or perhaps they'll be able to pick up another property at a good price.

Tips for Opening a B&B

The business owners in this chapter have found success—and paradise—in the B&B business. If you think that B&B ownership sounds interesting to you, consider the following tips as you get started:

Buy a Home You Love

When buying a property, don't settle on the best of a mediocre list. (For more about waiting for the right property, see Chapter 7.) Running a B&B is a quality of life decision, so make sure the property meets your hopes about where you want to live. If it doesn't, the little day-to-day tasks of running the business will become irritating and tiresome. "The thing we did right was buying a place that we love," Patricia says. "It is easy to get up every morning and do what you have to do when you love the property."

Consider Buying a B&B With an Existing Track Record and Clientele

If you are considering running a B&B business in a highly competitive market like Cape Cod, give yourself a head start by taking over an existing business. Because it takes years to build a reputation and client base, starting a new B&B is more difficult when competing in a market with many other established inns, especially if you are new to the business. However, if your chosen location is in a smaller market, especially one that has relatively low property values or is experiencing new growth in tourism, then buying a property and converting it into a B&B might make sense.

Referrals and Repeat Customers Are Your Bread and Butter

While Web listings are important, any B&B owner knows that most of their business comes from customers who return year after year, and refer their inns to family and friends. Showing a personal interest in customers is one way to keep them coming back, and can also be one of the most enjoyable aspects of running a B&B. "The best way we have to measure whether or not we're doing a good job is by how many repeat customers we have," Vince says. He then listed some of the guests staying at the inn at the time of his interview: "We have a couple staying with us today, and it's their fourth time here. And there are two sisters from Washington, DC, that come and stay with us every year. Having repeat customers is like having friends come to visit."

 FIND OUT MORE

Successful B&B owners know that the Internet is not only a powerful tool for marketing to their customers, but a great place for customers to give feedback. There's a myriad of blogs out there, like www.debfreakbast.com, which covers the B&B industry, including links to B&Bs for sale.

Read Up, and Take a Class

Around the country—especially in regions where inns are plentiful—local colleges and other organizations offer classes on how to run a B&B. The instructors are often experienced in the business and can impart valuable first-hand knowledge about what works and what doesn't. Many a headache can be avoided by taking such a class prior to buying your first B&B. Vince and Patricia said they regret never taking one; Cecily and Richard are glad they did.

Ask the Previous Owners to Train You

If you buy an existing business, take advantage of the previous owners' experience, as no one knows your B&B better than the people who have already been running it for years. Cecily and Richard made sure that the previous owners of the Isaiah Jones Homestead would be available to train them before committing to buying their first B&B. "They not only told us how to run things, they also gave us valuable information about their clients," Richard says.

Look at the B&B Through the Customers' Eyes

Patricia and Vince spend several days living in each of their six guest rooms during the slow season—sleeping in the bed, using the bathroom and shower, watching television, writing at the desk. "You don't realize what you need until you spend a few nights in the room," Vince says. "It gives you a better perspective—maybe the bed sucks, or the table doesn't work where it is, or the paint is chipping on the ceiling—details only a guest in the room would notice."

Have a Partner

There's a reason that most B&Bs are run by couples—it is hard work and far too much for one person alone. Many of the B&Bs that go out of business or are sold involve situations in which there is only one owner or one person in a partnership works outside the B&B. However, make sure that you define early the roles and responsibilities that each partner will assume. Clear job descriptions can help avoid pain later on in your business, and if you are more than business partners, your personal relationship.

Make Sure the Size Fits

Too many B&B owners get obsessed with increasing their occupancy rates without considering the corresponding increase in work. If your occupancy rate is 80% or 90%, but you're exhausted all the time, you probably need to raise your prices and bring your occupancy rates down to a more manageable 60% to 70%. Many B&B owners fail to take into account their own health, and end up having to hire help or cancel bookings because they become ill or too exhausted to manage the business. For sake of comparison, the average national annual occupancy rate for all B&Bs is only about 40%. However, that percentage averages all seasons of the year, and the difference in occupancy rates between seasons varies widely.

Have an Exit Strategy

The best time to get started on an exit strategy for your B&B is before purchasing it. (For considerations about how to fit your business plan into your overall financial plan, see Chapter 13.) Consider how long you plan on owning the property and whether selling it will be part of your strategy. If so, do some homework on the resale market in the area you are considering. Reviewing sales of B&B properties will give you an idea of how long you may need to hold a property to earn a suitable profit, and what physical characteristics seem to be most valued. With this in mind, you will be more informed in choosing a B&B property, and gain a better understanding of which features of any candidate property will need to be updated, replaced, or restored to earn the greatest profit on resale. ●

A Tale of Three Wineries

While bed and breakfasts are certainly among the most popular small businesses in paradise, owning a winery is also near the top of many people's lists of dream occupations. The vision of pouring your latest vintage for guests at your zinfandel vineyard is a dream for hundreds, if not thousands, of us—this author included!

As mentioned in Chapter 1, there are now more than 5,000 wineries in America—up from less than 3,000 wineries in 2000—and they are not only located in California. Wineries have sprouted up in all 50 states, including Alaska and Hawaii. At first glance, the number of existing wineries may be off-putting—evidence of a crowded, highly competitive market where there's no room for newcomers. But here is the good news: While the number of wineries has shot up, so has the demand for wine (see "Americans Are Drinking More Wine," below).

Americans Are Drinking More Wine

One out of every three Americans drinks wine, according to the Wine Institute. That's up from one in six just 20 years ago. Since 2000 alone, some 25 million more people have started drinking wine in the United States, and the growth does not show any signs of slowing.

In fact, the U.S. market consumes much more wine than it produces. Compare that with the European market, which still produces 50% of the world's wine but cannot consume anywhere near that level of production. Other countries such as Chile, Argentina, Australia, and South Africa have stepped in to help meet demand from wine-thirsty U.S. consumers. While other countries have been helping satisfy the demand of the U.S. market, there is still room for growth in domestic production.

"The next 20 years will be the greatest era in the history of American wines," predicts Vic Motto, an investment banker to the wine industry and chief executive officer of Global Wine Partners LLC. Motto predicts much of the growth in U.S. production will come from small independent producers. His prediction is based in part on industry growth patterns which show higher-priced wines becoming more popular in the U.S. than low-priced ones. (See "Tastes Are Getting More Expensive," below.)

Tastes Are Getting More Expensive

In the 1990s, low-priced wine of $8 per bottle or less was by far the biggest segment in the industry, and those wines are produced primarily by large, mass-producing winemakers. A small independent winery can't make a profit by selling wine for $2 a bottle, such as the famed "two-buck Chuck" sold at Trader Joe's stores. However, sales of low-priced wine started slowing in 2000, while sales of midpriced wines ($8 to $15 per bottle), have continued to grow. Simultaneously, high-priced wines of $15 or more have been the fastest-growing segment of the market, with sales increasing at an average annual rate of 20% for the past 15 years.

In 2005, high-priced wines represented the largest segment of the U.S. market for the first time, and appear poised to hold that leadership position for the foreseeable future. That growth favors small producers, who can make a profit selling wine at higher prices and who appeal to the eclectic tastes of today's wine consumers.

"There are still some people out there who want apple pies baked one at a time instead of 4,000 at a time. It's the same in the wine industry," says Steve Reynolds, a former dentist who now owns and manages the Reynolds Family Winery in Napa Valley.

Mulan Chan, a wine buyer for K&L Wine Merchants in San Francisco, says most of the consumers who come through K&L's doors are looking for more than just good wine at a good price. "They're looking for a story," she says, explaining that customers tend to shy away from big-name wineries and favor instead a small label with an interesting background or unique method of making or marketing its wines. She noted that consumers are becoming increasingly adventurous in their tastes and willing to try wines from areas outside of main growing regions such as California's Napa Valley and France's Bordeaux region.

How do you go about starting your own winery, and managing it to success? Two things are certain: First, it's not an easy business to break into, so if you're not passionate about it, you are not likely to succeed. Second, there is no single path toward success—every successful winemaker today has a unique story. Perhaps there is no better example of how differently people get their start in the wine business than by comparing the genesis of three little wineries located within half a mile of each other in Dry Creek Valley: David Coffaro Winery, Talty Vineyards, and Dutcher Crossing Winery.

Just 90 minutes north of San Francisco, Dry Creek Valley is one of those bucolic, off-the-beaten-path regions that wine enthusiasts love to keep secret. Populated with family-run vineyards and landscaped with meandering creeks, it offers the serenity Napa Valley did 30 years ago, before today's big crowds and $20 wine tastings.

David Coffaro:
Start by Growing the Best Grapes

Long before Google, Yahoo!, or even Apple or Microsoft, David Coffaro was investing in initial public offerings (IPOs). He started his career as a research assistant at a San Francisco brokerage house, earning $400 a month. At a time when Silicon Valley was still farmland and called Santa Clara Valley, David became an expert on the IPO market and technology startups.

David eventually made enough money to quit his job and open his own investment firm in a small office in San Rafael, just north of San Francisco, investing primarily for himself and family and friends. IPOs continued to be his specialty, and much of his time was spent talking investment banks into letting him get on their new-issue distribution lists—not an easy task, since at that time most IPO shares were reserved for well-to-do investors at large brokerage houses. He loved to take risks, and it usually paid off. He married his wife Patricia in 1973, bought a new home in nearby Fairfax, California, and life was good.

In 1979, however, David's world crashed. While on vacation in Santa Barbara, he risked all of his money—and that of others—on a single investment in an upstart technology company, Advanced Micro Devices. While AMD later went on to become a Silicon Valley success story, a sharp drop in its price at the time forced David to cash in all of his own shares to cover the losses of the other investors. Financially, he was completely wiped out.

Returning home, he assessed his future and realized he no longer had the stomach for the investment business. He had long been a wine aficionado, and now he began to wonder about a career in the wine business.

"I decided I needed a new job, and wine was something I always found interesting," David said. Not wanting to stray too far from home, he drove north to explore Sonoma and Napa counties. As he recalls: "Unfortunately, I quickly found out that jobs in the wine industry don't pay well."

On a whim, he wondered what it would take to buy a vineyard, so he looked up Rich Thomas, a well-known viticulturalist and professor at Santa Rosa Junior College, in the heart of Sonoma County. Thomas sent him to Midtown Realty in Healdsburg. Less than an hour after leaving Thomas' office, he was staring at a 25-acre vineyard that would become his life for the next 28 years (and counting).

"I went from having the idea to buy a vineyard to finding the vineyard I would eventually own all in one day," David says.

However, convincing his wife to make the move was not easy. "I grew up on a dairy farm, and I moved to San Francisco to get out of the country," Patricia says. "When he told me about his idea to buy a vineyard, I thought, 'Oh great!' I didn't want to go. And besides, David didn't know anything about farming. He didn't even know what to do with a tractor."

Patricia also had an established job as a legal secretary in San Rafael. Still, she agreed to make the move. "I guess she still loved me back then," David now jokes. (See Chapter 6, "Check With Those Closest to You," for more about working with partners and family members in your small business in paradise.)

It took about four months to actually close the deal on the vineyard. "Nobody would give me a loan. I had no experience farming and had never been on a tractor." The vineyard he chose was 25 acres, with a small 1,100-square-foot home on it and about nine acres of existing zinfandel vines. There was no winery, and no winemaking equipment. The Coffaros sold their Fairfax home for $73,000, used $70,000 of that as a down payment on the property, and put the remaining $3,000 toward start-up costs. For the next 16 years, the Coffaros were grape growers.

From the beginning of the venture, David found the people of Dry Creek Valley welcoming and happy to help their new neighbors. They were quick to share advice on getting started, and later helped him find markets for his grapes. He also got some help from Patricia's father, who occasionally made the three-hour trek from Modesto, California, to show David how to farm and prune vines. Fortunately for the Coffaros, the previous owner of the vineyard had an agreement to sell the entire harvest to the Gallo family, which at that time controlled most of the wine production in Sonoma County. By continuing that arrangement, Coffaro was able to earn income without the interruption sometimes associated with a change in business ownership. Additionally, he learned more about growing grapes, as Gallo generously offered invaluable expertise and advice. (For more about the advantages of buying an existing business, see Chapter 12, "Buying a Business Versus Starting From Scratch.")

Eventually seeking to diversify the types of grapes he grew, Coffaro started planting sauvignon blanc and cabernet sauvignon—two up-and-coming varietals—in the early 1980s. Once the harvests were ready, however, the buyer David had anticipated would buy the grapes decided it didn't want them. Faced with a possible loss, he needed to quickly find other buyers and turned to his neighbors. Nearby Preston Vineyards, for instance, one of the biggest sauvignon blanc producers in the area, ended up buying much of that and subsequent sauvignon blanc harvests. In the meantime, David kept selling the zinfandel grapes to Gallo.

For the next decade, Coffaro worked the fields, learning every aspect of growing grapes for wine (see "A Year of Hard Labor," below). Selling grapes was also a learning experience. If the sugar content of the grapes wasn't exactly right, buyers would either turn them down completely or offer him a much lower price. David recalls: "Gallo looked for about 24% sugar content for the zinfandel grapes. Preston wanted between 21.5% and 22% for sauvignon blanc, and would drop the price by 1.5% for every tenth of a percentage point over 22% sugar content. The first year I sold to Preston I came in at 22.2% and got docked 3% of the price. After that, I was right in the middle of their range."

A Year of Hard Labor

David Coffaro's annual work cycle was typical of the work required in growing grapes: "The hardest thing I ever did was the pruning," he said. Every day, in late winter and early spring, he spent four hours in the morning and another two hours in late afternoon pruning the vines himself. He would strip off the previous year's growth—usually about six feet of vine that was wrapped around the trellises—readying the vines for the next season. When that was done, it was time to "sulfur" the vines to prevent mildew, which entailed spraying a fine mist of sulfur from a blower strapped to his back throughout the entire vineyard (like most wineries, he now owns a machine that does this). After sulfuring, each vine would then have to be "trained"—or tied in position—on the trellises. In July and August, the work would ease up a bit until harvest season, at least on the established vines, but there was still plenty to do on the 12 acres of new vines that David had planted. Finally, harvest time arrived, and again the work increased—this time picking the grapes and preparing them for shipment.

Meanwhile, Patricia kept working in San Rafael for the first few years, making the hour-long commute each way, every day. "I didn't do any of the physical labor at the vineyard," she says. "I just stayed inside and pretended I was still in the city. It took me a while to really appreciate it here." Then, in the late eighties, they started a family and had two daughters. "The vineyard was a great place to raise a family," Patricia says.

In 1993, David turned 50, and the risk-taker in him emerged again. He was approached by an investor who wanted to open a winery on David's property, and the two formed a partnership. This time, though, taking the risk didn't pay off. The partnership soured, and a harvest was almost wasted because an agreement about bottling the wine they had produced fell through. In the end, David managed to find a bulk wine producer to purchase the wine, but at a much lower return than he had anticipated from bottling the wine at Coffaro Winery.

What Is Bulk Wine?

Much of the wine made in the U.S. is purchased in bulk from other winemakers and "cellared and bottled" by the winery on the label. Producing bulk wine is an intermediate step between growing grapes and bottling your own wine, but because margins are small, meaningful profits can usually only be made with large-scale production.

While the partnership ended on a sour note, it offered David his first experience in producing wine, and inspired him to start his own winery. He took out a loan, and began to buy the equipment and secure the licenses needed to transition from grape grower to winery.

At the time, the transition costs from vineyard to winery for a small grower such as David were about $100,000. (Now the same conversion would likely cost double that amount.) Of those costs, $24,000 was for a new septic system to process wine waste, which Sonoma County required in order to approve David's plans. The remaining funds were spent on a wine press, processing equipment, barrels, and a storage facility.

With the little winery up and running, and the kids now in school, Patricia quit her job and began working with David full time. From the small office attached to their house, Patricia helped manage the books, handled order fulfillment, and did the event planning, all of which she continues to do today. (See Chapter 11 for more about the importance of event planning for small businesses in paradise). Like the couples who run B&Bs, David and Patricia share duties according to their own skill sets and interests—David manages the business and is the face that most customers see, while Patricia runs the back office.

A SMALL BUSINESS IN *Paradise*

If you would like to learn more about the David Coffaro Winery, go to www.coffaro.com.

From the beginning of his winemaking career, David wanted to specialize in blends of his best grapes, so he bottled a zinfandel-cabernet blend and an "estate cuvee" which represented "a blend of the best grapes grown in Dry Creek Valley." In September 1995, the estate cuvee won a gold medal at the Sonoma County Harvest Fair, and word quickly spread of the quality of the Coffaros' wine.

David recalls: "At the time, the Internet was just getting going. CompuServe had a good wine site that was frequented by some young wine enthusiasts. My name was mentioned, and demand shot up."

The David Coffaro Winery produced only 427 cases in its first year. Now, the Coffaros bottle 5,000 cases—most of which are sold in advance to avid customers. "We have a broker in San Francisco who distributes to some retailers, but most of our sales are through word of mouth. We don't do any marketing."

A small sign on the road displays the name of the winery. There are no fixed tasting hours and no separate tasting room, but if you stop by, David will be glad to pour you several tastes at a counter in the wine storage facility, which resembles an oversized tin garage.

Looking back, he's glad he made the switch to making wine when he did. If he had done so sooner, he would not have had grape growing experience, which he counts as invaluable. If he had not made the switch, however, he would not enjoy the increased profitability of making wine as compared to growing grapes. In terms of profitability, he says there really is no comparison. For example, David can sell his grapes to make one bottle of wine for about $3.60, at a cost of goods sold of about $2. But if he makes his own wine, he can sell it for $15 to $20 a bottle, at a cost-of-goods-sold of about $8.50.

What now for the Coffaros? David says he's had enough career changes for one lifetime. "And Patricia is finally agreeing that we may just make a buck on this little winery." So they'll keep on doing what they're doing, probably well past the age at which most people retire.

 FIND OUT MORE

Tap the industry barrel for information by visiting www.winebusiness. com, a leading online authority for winemakers and sellers. The website has extensive real estate and classified ad sections, and is the publisher of *Wine Business Monthly*, an industry magazine. There are also plenty of blogs online, detailing days in the life of a winemaker or merchant, such as http://blog.selenewines.com and www.steepcreek. blogspot.com

Talty Vineyards: Make the Best Wine

Growing grapes is one way to start in the wine business; making wine is another. The latter was the route taken by Michael Talty, owner and winemaker of Talty Vineyards & Winery, which is just a stone's throw down Dry Creek Road from David Coffaro's place.

"I'm a wine grower, not a grape grower," Michael says, "and there's a big difference." Talty puts the same amount of care and precision into the process and production of a bottle of wine as Coffaro does into caring for his grapes. The result is two widely different styles of wine. For example, Talty focuses exclusively on making the best bottle of zinfandel he can, while Coffaro concentrates on selecting the best grapes he can of several different varietals, and then combining them into one bottle of wine.

A SMALL BUSINESS IN *Paradise*

If you would like to learn more about Talty Vineyards & Winery, go to www.taltyvineyards.com.

The William Talty Vineyard is named after Michael's father, who Michael says was "very influential in my life." William introduced Michael to wine at an early age. First touring Dry Creek Valley in the early 1970s, father William became a zinfandel aficionado, touring the wine country several times a year. By the early 1980s, he was bringing Michael with him.

Michael recalls, "One year I decided that, since I could cook, I could probably make wine, too. In the late 1980s, I bought some grapes, and a friend and I made a barrel of wine in his basement." He bought the oak barrels straight from the producer, Demptos of Napa, a subsidiary of the famed French barrel maker. (Michael was pleasantly surprised that Demptos would sell single barrels to a small producer.) He bought the grapes from a broker he found by reading the bulletin board at the wine supply shop where he bought his fermentation supplies, paying about $750 for a half-ton of grapes. (Now the same quantity of grapes would likely cost almost double that amount.)

The production later moved to his garage, and one barrel became two per year, then three, then as many as 12. The result, Michael recalls, "wasn't very good, and we didn't sell any of it. But we had fun making it and drinking it." Michael was hooked and began reading more about winemaking. While he already had a business degree from San Jose State, a friend introduced him to the extension program at the University of California–Davis, one of the foremost agriculture and viticulture programs in the country. He started taking classes, and according to Michael, "My wines started getting pretty decent."

Michael's father, the zinfandel enthusiast, suggested Michael purchase some zinfandel grapes from the Dry Creek Valley, which many, including William Talty, considered to be the best zinfandel-growing region in Northern California.

"In 1993, I embarked on a quest to get Dry Creek Valley zinfandel grapes, but found that none were available. All the independent growers had already promised their entire crops to the wineries. They weren't going to sell grapes to a home wine producer. So my Dad said, 'Maybe we should buy our own little vineyard.'"

A few weeks later, William Talty had a heart attack while exercising at the gym. Sadly, he passed away, and what had been a hobby for Michael Talty then became a quest. The Talty family business—a court reporting service in San Jose, California—was founded by William Talty and after his death, Michael took over its operation. But he never forgot his father's dream of buying a vineyard—a dream that had now become his own. He started to look around, but vineyard property seemed too expensive.

Michael kept looking, however—staying in touch with agents, getting to know local winery owners, and visiting Dry Creek Valley as often as possible. Finally, in 1997, he seized on a real estate opportunity, trading up a family-owned storage facility for a small, six-acre vineyard in Dry Creek Valley. The deal, structured as a like-kind exchange under the Internal Revenue Code, allowed Michael to exchange a large equity stake in the small storage facility for a small equity stake in the much-more-expensive vineyard. The remainder of the purchase price was financed. The vineyard was not only planted 100% with zinfandel vines, but they were old and head-pruned and grown on a nonirrigated field, which according to Michael, requires more upkeep but makes much better wine. (Unless it is done with extreme care, irrigation can harm vines, which is why the practice of irrigating fields is banned in many regions of the old winemaking world, such as Bordeaux.)

What Is a Like-Kind Exchange?

In general, Section 1031 of the Internal Revenue Code allows the owner of business or investment property to exchange that property for other property like it without recognizing a gain or loss on the transaction. Therefore, if you own a business property (like Michael Talty's storage facility) and that property has appreciated in value while you have owned it, you could exchange it for a different business property (like Michael's vineyard) without recognizing any taxable gain on the exchange. There are many rules to follow in doing these transactions, and there are businesses whose primary mission is to structure what are known as 1031 exchanges. Check online for these businesses—simply type "1031 exchange" into your search engine. See the Internal Revenue Service website as well for the rules relating to 1031 exchanges: www.irs.gov.

Michael's plan was to make wine. But he still had a court reporting company to manage, and a wife, Katie, and three children who were all entrenched in life in San Jose.

"I used to come up here one day a week, and that was my favorite day of the week. The more I came here, the more I disliked what I did in San Jose."

Michael worked the vineyard himself, selling most of the grapes to other wineries in the first few years. But each year, he brought some of the grapes home to San Jose, where he made increasing quantities of wine in his own basement. Then, in 2001, he built a winery on the vineyard site. Most of the equipment came from his garage—a press, a "stemmer," and a dozen barrels. Still, Michael estimates his total investment in converting the vineyard to a winery was about $500,000—including the buildings, use permits, septic system, additional barrels, and other miscellaneous items. In that same year, Michael and his family moved to the vineyard, first living in the winery building while a new home was being built.

FIND OUT MORE

Read a business plan or two online to see how others started their wine business. Search for "vineyard business" or "winery business" in your favorite search engine, or look at the extensive business plan posted by Cornell economics students here: http://aem.cornell. edu/outreach/extensionpdf/eb0207.pdf. For a discussion of business plans, see also "Write a Business Plan—Really," in Chapter 6.

"Nothing went right," Katie remembers. "We had this big master plan and it all fell apart." Their home in San Jose took a year to sell, so they couldn't even get started on their new home right away.

"We had to turn our wine office into an apartment for our family," says Katie. "It was a 600-square-foot, one-bedroom apartment. I called it 'rack 'em, stack 'em' living. It was supposed to be just for a little while, but it turned out to take over two years to complete."

Finally, they sold the court reporting business and moved into their new home. For the first time, the Talty family was entirely financially dependent on the winery. "It was a big unknown," Katie remembers. "Plus, we left our extended families in San Jose. For me, that was leaving behind my support system."

Like David Coffaro, Michael lists administrative red tape as one of the biggest challenges to getting started as a winery. "There are a lot of compliance issues and reporting requirements with federal and state agencies related to the production of alcohol." (See "Registrations, Licenses, and Permits" in Chapter 12 for an introduction to obtaining governmental approvals.)

There are, however, ways to avoid some of the compliance headaches. "You don't have to have your own production facility," he points out. "You can have your wine made at someone else's facility and work under their bond." (See "Tips for Opening Your Winery" at the end of the chapter.) "But then you don't have as much control over the winemaking."

Like Patricia Coffaro, it took Katie Talty some time to accept living full-time in Dry Creek Valley. But with a background in sales and marketing, she quickly became Michael's business partner, and now handles not only sales and marketing but much of the order fulfillment for the winery as well.

"Our marketing is mainly just word of mouth at this point," says Katie. "In the beginning, we tried to get into wine shops and restaurants. I would line up with the herd of cattle—other producers—who each had 15 bottles to show, and I'm standing there with my one bottle of wine. They would all say it's a great wine, but nobody has heard of you." Word of mouth has worked so far, but as their wine becomes better known, the Taltys say they plan to increase marketing efforts again, possibly starting a wine club.

Like the Coffaros, the Taltys have had their ups and downs in the wine business, with a near disaster in 2004. Most California wineries sterilize the grapes harvested from the vineyards, and then inject them with cultured yeast for fermentation. "I don't do that," Michael says. "I use natural yeast from the vineyard, because it improves the flavor." But natural yeast can be volatile, as Michael discovered in 2004 when he faced a "stuck fermentation" crisis. Stuck fermentation is a common winemaking problem that occurs when, for various reasons, the fermenting process stops before the sugar is sufficiently converted to alcohol. Unless the fermentation process can be restarted, the result is usually poor-tasting wine.

"I walked into the house one night and told Katie, 'We're in trouble.'" Michael credits his own problem-solving skills, honed during 22 years of managing a court reporting business, in figuring out how to solve the fermentation problem and salvage the vintage. Rather than giving up on the harvest and settling for a bad-tasting wine, Michael enlisted the help of local winemakers he trusted and also did some of his own research, finally coming up with a method to successfully restart the fermentation process.

What now for the winery? Michael explains: "My goal is to produce 2,000 cases per year. We're at about 1,200 now. I worked out that if we can sell 2,000 cases annually, we can earn a living. We wouldn't be rolling in dough, but we can put the kids through college and take one vacation a year. The real bounty is being able to live here, in paradise."

Dutcher Crossing: Buy the Best of Everything

Knowing how to grow suitable grapes and make distinctive wines are surely two important aspects of the winery business. But they are not everything. Bruce Nevins and Jim Stevens are proving that the foundation of a good winery can be laid with business savvy, merchandising skills—and some money.

That is not to say that they don't make great wine. They do! But they outsourced both the growing of the grapes and the making of the wine to some of the best experts in the business, using the business skills they have already developed to found and manage a successful winery.

Bruce and Jim are best known for introducing bottled water to the American public. They founded Perrier North America in 1976 and directed the merchandising of the bottled water around the United States and Canada. Later, they acquired both Poland Springs on the East Coast and Calistoga on the West Coast, further cementing their reputations as the kings of bottled water. Along the way, though, they also distributed wine, mostly for European producers such as Italy's Bollini and Castello Di Gabbiano, along with some French winemakers.

In the early 1980s, Bruce and Jim sold their interests in the bottled water business, and each took an executive-level position at a multinational corporation—Bruce as managing director of Reebok's international group, and Jim as chief operating officer at Coca-Cola.

In 1991, Bruce made his first foray into vineyard ownership, buying a vineyard in the Alexander Valley, just 20 miles east of where his and Jim's future winery—Dutcher Crossing—is now located. He hired Tri-Valley Vineyard Management, an important player in the Sonoma wine industry, to grow the grapes and maintain the fields. Tri-Valley manages several vineyards in the area, and usually makes most of the agricultural decisions, such as when to prune the grapes and when to harvest, leaving the owners to manage the rest of the business. Bruce sold the grapes to other wineries, such as Ferrari-Carrano, one of the biggest in Dry Creek Valley and now a neighbor of Dutcher Crossing.

A SMALL BUSINESS IN *Paradise*

If you are interested in learning more about Dutcher Crossing Winery, visit www.dutchercrossing winery.com.

Like many entrepreneurs who start a business in paradise as a part-time venture, Bruce found himself wanting to be in Dry Creek full time. He continued to work for Reebok, but in the late 1990s started making plans to build a house on the property at Alexander Valley, which is separated from Dry Creek Valley by Highway 101. "Our intention was to grow grapes and be involved in the community." Bruce retired from Reebok and moved into the new home with his family in 2000. "My wife, Sindy, and I had talked about it for years. Part of the appeal was the fun of growing grapes."

Like Coffaro, Bruce was introduced to viticulturalist Rich Thomas and took his class at Santa Rosa Junior College. Wine production and grape growing started to become more than just a business venture to him, and he became more involved in his own vineyard. "At that point, we started to think it could be interesting to get into the winemaking business."

Meanwhile, former partner Jim Stevens was now retired and considering his own plans to move to the Sonoma wine country. In 2001, the two formed a partnership and bought Dutcher Crossing—a 32-acre plot with 27 acres of vineyards. There were no buildings, except a small pruning shed and an old cottage. Jim later built a home on the property, where he now spends part of the year.

They immediately began plans for establishing the winery. They hired Tri-Valley Vineyard Management again to manage and harvest the vineyard, and construction was begun on a new winery and tasting room. Meanwhile, they sold shares in the winery to private investors to help finance the project. And they hired Kerry Damskey, one of the most respected winemakers in the Napa-Sonoma area, as their chief winemaker.

Dutcher Crossing's first commercial vintage in 2005 produced about 2,000 cases, all of which was sold directly to consumers. In spite of their own skills as large-scale beverage distributors, Bruce and Jim wanted to grow sales through word of mouth, and focused on building personal relationships with people who can promote their wines.

The second harvest—in 2006—yielded more than twice the number of cases than the first harvest. They produce a wide selection of wines, including zinfandels, syrah, petit syrah, cabernet sauvignon, several blends, and soon, sauvignon blanc.

Bruce says that making good wines is the most important component of Dutcher Crossing's success. Indeed, he said the years of merchandising experience that both he and Jim brought to the business have served them much less than they expected in building the winery. While it was important to focus on what they do best, and to hire others with expertise to run the vineyards and make the wine, it was also important for Bruce and Jim to learn as much as they could about growing grapes and making wine.

What now for Dutcher Crossing? "Steady as she goes," Bruce says. His goal is to reach annual sales of about 9,000 to 10,000 cases, and then maintain that level. As for Bruce, he's building a new home near Dry Creek Valley and plans to continue managing Dutcher Crossing well into retirement.

Tips for Opening Your Winery

As you can see from the stories in this chapter, the winemaking business has many facets. Are you still thinking about making your own wine? If so, here are some tips to consider:

Do It Right Instead of Fast

As a small winery owner, you're not going to be successful by trying to compete with the big guys in marketing, distribution, or production. Producing good wine, and getting it recognized, is the key to your success. For Michael Talty, the reward for his hard work came when a team of *Wall Street Journal* wine critics toured Napa and Sonoma counties and chose Talty's zinfandel as the best in the region. Talty is so passionate about his winemaking that he restricts the amount of fruit on the vines in order to intensify flavors, and discards many of the remaining grapes if they don't meet his meticulous standards. "Grape growers come by and see fruit on the floor of my winery, and they scratch their heads." For David Coffaro, doing it right meant learning to grow good grapes before making the transition to winemaking. "If you make a decent wine, people will find you," says David. "The knowledge you get from planting a vineyard and making wine as an amateur is invaluable." Making wine is an art form, and takes not only firsthand experience, but an education in viticulture. If you don't have both of those, make sure you hire someone who does.

Location, Location, Location

"They say location is everything, and that's not far from the truth in the wine business," says Michael Talty. Of course, buying a vineyard in an area that is known to produce good wine grapes is crucial. Before buying any property, however, make sure to have the soil tested by a commercial soil-testing laboratory to make sure it is conducive to grape production. (Keep in mind that such tests are usually best when the soil is moist and not frozen.) If you want to not only grow grapes but also build a winery, make sure it is located in a place wine drinkers want to visit. Michael cites his front entrance on Dry Creek Valley Road, and his strategic location between other major wineries, as key to his initial success. For more about choosing the location for your small business in paradise, see Chapter 7.

Get Your Name Out There

As the entrepreneurs in this chapter have illustrated, word of mouth is the best way for a small winery to make itself known. "Utilize relationship marketing," says Bruce Nevins. As in any business, you need to create advocates for your product, a base of people who like your wine and winery enough to recommend them to their friends. If you have a tasting room, make visiting it an enjoyable event rather than just a place to shop for wine. "Katie and I remember what it's like to be on the other side of the table when wine tasting," says Michael Talty. "The places we liked most were those with the friendliest people, where the owners were pouring the wine. Somehow it makes the wine taste better." Entering tasting contests is a great way to fuel interest, especially when getting started. Use the Internet. Get involved with local events. "We are involved with local wine events during the off season," says Coffaro, adding that a cooperative marketing group called the Russian River Wine Road has organized barrel tastings and other events to promote local wineries. "That removes a lot of the seasonality from the wine business." (While consumers drink wine year-round, they don't visit wineries year-round. And since most of the sales of small new wineries are made on site, business tends to thrive during the fall and spring months and slow during the winter and summer.) See Chapter 11 for more about community events.

Manage Your Costs Well

Keep in mind that wine takes time to cultivate, ferment, and age. It's not an overnight process. As a result, it's important to pace your costs with your anticipated revenue. "You really have to look at capital costs, including equipment, facilities, and a tasting room, and then you have to look at recurring costs and inventory. For instance, red wine needs to be stored for at least two years, white for only a year," says Bruce Nevins. Michael Talty, who estimates he spent $500,000 to build his winery–in addition to the cost of buying the vineyard—warns of the unknown: "You never know when there's going to be a bad harvest or a change in demand." Having a financial cushion is important, whether it's money in the bank, an available line of credit, or a second job if things get rough. See Chapter 13 about managing the risk of starting a new business.

Don't Get Fancy Right Away

When getting started, produce grapes and wines that have an established market. Growing exotic wine varietals such as malbec, dolcetto, or primitivo can be exciting, but their demand can come and go, whereas the major varietals such as cabernet sauvignon, merlot, and chardonnay enjoy a much more stable level of demand.

Hire the Right People

Recognizing that quality (both in wine and winemakers) is important, Bruce Nevins made a point of hiring one of the best winemakers he could find. David Coffaro says it's possible to operate a winery with only two people—a winemaker and a cellar chief. If you're on a budget, and just starting out, consider hiring your winemaker straight out of one of the top programs such as University of California–Davis, Fresno State University, Washington State University, or Cornell University. The program at UC Davis combines both viticulture (the growing of grapes) with enology (the science of winemaking), with a good dose of business management thrown in as well. A good cellar chief, who will do most of the work involved with storing the wine and topping the barrels, can be hired away from an assistant position at another winery. If opening a tasting room, Bruce Nevins posits that a third key position to be filled is that of a tasting room manager, and requires someone who not only knows something about wine but knows how to sell it, has worked in the service industry, and has a personality suited to meeting and greeting guests.

Beware of Red Tape

Both Michael Talty and David Coffaro sited regulatory issues as one of the biggest challenges to opening a winery. If you plan only to buy a vineyard, there are few regulatory hurdles. But if you plan to start producing wine—whether at your own or someone else's facility—you will need to comply with a host of federal—and likely local—rules. The federal government regulates wine production through the Alcohol and Tobacco Tax and Trade Bureau of the U.S. Treasury Department. The agency's website at www.ttb.gov (click on the "wine" tab) is packed with free information about legal requirements for different types of wine producers, Web-based tutorials, and announcements about upcoming free seminars in most of the big winemaking regions. While many new wine owners hire lawyers or other professionals to handle federal compliance issues, David says government regulators are accessible and can be helpful in getting you started. The other major regulatory hurdle for wine producers is compliance with local and county ordinances, especially regarding disposal of winery waste. Most regions require a separate, professionally installed septic system be installed before local approvals to build a production facility are given.

Learn Management Skills

In the end, a winery is a business, and entrepreneurial and management skills are essential. "You have to be skilled in small business management," says Michael Talty. "I ran a small business for 22 years, and I studied it in college. There's no way I could have been successful without that background." The particular skills which he brought to the wine business included managing relationships with vendors, supply management, and regulatory compliance. See Chapter 6 for more about getting prepared for your own small business in paradise.

Consider Investors

While it is gratifying to build a winery on your own, using your own funds or lines of credit, consider bringing in other investors. They not only bring money, but they become advocates for your wine. The founders of Dutcher Crossing chose investors who contributed dollars and geographical diversity, the latter of which helps spread the word about the wine. "That's why we have investors from all over—Florida, Colorado, Southern California, New York, and Boston. They are all advocates," says Bruce Nevins.

For the Love of Wine . . .

Like most small businesses in paradise, the rewards of winemaking are not necessarily financial (although they can be), but often are related to lifestyle—the possibility of combining earning a livelihood with a life on a vineyard, an escape from city life, the pleasure of creating something tangible, and literally enjoying the fruits of your labor. But it is not for everyone, as Michael Talty advises: "I would not recommend that anyone start a winery unless they are passionate about wine. There is not a tremendous amount of financial reward in this industry, but if you have that passion, it's awesome. I can truly say I love what I do. And I love to get up and do it every day. It's about the dream, not the money."

When Paradise Calls

Chapters 2 and 3 described two types of small businesses—wineries and bed and breakfasts—that many people dream of starting. However, many owners of small businesses in paradise never imagined they would be where they are today, doing what they're doing. That does not mean they haven't found paradise, but instead shows that it can be found in many forms, and the road there can be full of twists and turns.

This chapter will look at the owners of three businesses—two individuals and one couple, whose involvement in their businesses represents a radical shift from their prior work lives (or in one instance, a concurrent career). Their experiences in being called—or pushed—to paradise may inspire you to recognize and act on opportunities that come your way.

Someone Else's Dream ... Your Paradise

On California's famed Highway One, about two hours north of San Francisco, sits the little town of Bodega Bay. On the bluff overlooking the Pacific Ocean, just as you're entering town, is a charming little store called "Candy & Kites." In front, there's always a colorful collection of kites, windsocks, and garden spinners, and inside, some of the best saltwater taffy you'll ever taste. Candy & Kites is impossible to miss, and the first thing that comes to mind when seeing it is, "What a great idea for a store. And what a great location."

Candy & Kites was the dream of Roma Robbins and Barbara Price—two well-known local residents who founded it in 1983 and ran it until their retirement in 2003. However, since 2003, Candy & Kites has been the small business in paradise of Fiona and David Love, neither of whom ever expected to be in Bodega Bay, selling candy and kites.

Fiona and David spent most of their work lives in the hotel business—David in various management roles at Westin, and later with Marriott; Roma in sales and office administration, also for national chains. They both worked long hours, so much so that in 2001 they decided to quit their jobs and take off on a ten-month bicycle trip from Vancouver to

San Francisco, and then throughout Australia and New Zealand—all of it on a tandem (two-seater) bicycle.

They had barely returned from their trip when Fiona got an email from an old friend, Roma Robbins' daughter Nicki, asking if they wanted to buy Candy & Kites. Fiona and Nicki had been friends since they attended high school together in Marin County (north of San Francisco). Fiona and David had known Roma and Barbara for years, and had visited the store on numerous occasions. "Of course we thought she was kidding—as it turned out, she wasn't," Fiona said.

A SMALL BUSINESS IN Paradise

If you would like to know more about Candy & Kites and its products, visit www.candyandkites.com. Better yet, visit the store!

At the time, David and Fiona were living in Oakland and contemplating going back to work in the hotel industry. Without the taste of paradise that the bicycle trip had given them, they might never have considered the offer to buy Candy & Kites. As it was, they decided to think about it. Would they enjoy running their own business? Would they be good at it? Could they handle the isolation of Bodega Bay? To answer these questions and learn more about the business, they convinced Roma and Barbara to let them work in the store on weekends. After six months of weekend experience, Fiona and David had satisfactorily resolved their doubts and took ownership of the store. (See Chapter 6 for more about deciding whether you would enjoy a particular business and location.)

What Kind of Retailer Are You?

If you just know you'd make a splash in retail but aren't sure what kind of business would fit you best, check out the multitude of possibilities in *Start Your Own Successful Retail Business* (Entrepreneur).

They quickly realized that their years in the hotel business gave them a big advantage in their work at Candy & Kites. "The hotel business can be pretty thankless, and there are a lot of long hours, but you get an amazing amount of training in customer service," Fiona says. "Today you hear a lot of complaints that customer service isn't what it used to be. But at most high-end hotels, making the customer happy is something they drill through your head."

David and Fiona took that experience to Candy & Kites and quickly implemented new customer service standards, including eliminating the store's no-return policy. "Now, if customers want to return something, we will either give them their money back or exchange it. Goodwill goes a long way, especially in a small business, because there is a lot of competition out there."

FIND OUT MORE

CandyBusiness magazine (www.retailmerchandising.net/cbus) covers all aspects of being a candy retailer, from protecting your sweet innovations in candy, to Food and Drug Administration alerts and guidelines, to writing a good business plan.

Unlike many couples who start small businesses, Fiona and David had no trouble falling into comfortable complementary roles at Candy & Kites. Says Fiona: "After 20 years of marriage, 15 years of working together in the hotel industry, and ten months together on a tandem bicycle, there wasn't much else to test in our marriage." David's strengths were in management and finance; Fiona's were in ordering, inventory, and organization. "We just fell into certain jobs," she says. However, they both enjoy working with customers—Fiona runs the front of the store where all the candy and toys are sold, and David manages the kite sales in the back. While they both had ample training in customer service, neither had spent time in direct customer sales, so making a sales pitch was something new to both of them. Over time, they each found their rhythm, and both found they enjoyed the sales process as well as the opportunity to meet people from around the world who stopped by their store.

David and Fiona have shown that you don't necessarily have to build a business for it to become your own personal paradise. They both say they probably couldn't have done it if they had to build the business from the ground up. (See "Buying a Business Versus Starting From Scratch" in Chapter 12 for more about this choice.) The fact that Candy & Kites had been up and running for 20 years made their job a lot easier—not only did it eliminate all the start-up headaches of a new business, but it also came with a ready-made base of return customers.

"It was still a big shock going from a steady paycheck to running your own business, but it would have been a lot more stressful if Candy & Kites wasn't an existing business," Fiona says.

Find a Fitting Franchise

Some people have a great idea; some people have a passion for business and a mind that puts that passion to work. If you're one of the latter, a franchise might be your perfect business. Whether it's a Subway or Big O Tires, you can research all sorts of options at www.franchising.com.

They have not changed the store much since buying it in 2003. "If it's not broken, don't fix it," Fiona says. They do, however, buy and sell more power kites (large kites designed to provide a lot of traction and often used to pull surfers, snowboarders, buggies, and so on), which Fiona attributes to her husband's presence and sales efforts: "I think guys like buying power kites from other guys." The couple also increased the amount of inventory in the front of the store. They admit owning their business is hard work—they get up every morning of every day throughout the year and fasten their kites, spinners, and windsocks to hooks and cables in the front yard. "That way customers always know we're open, even if it's raining."

A solid inventory of diverse and unique items is key to their success, Fiona says. "We shop around, we look at our competitors. If we see an item for sale at Toys'R'Us or Target, we don't want to carry it. We try to find unique items for our customers. And we try to work with vendors who will give us exclusive rights to sell their goods in Bodega Bay, especially since a second kite store recently opened down the street."

What next for Fiona and David? Fiona says they're building a house in Bodega Bay and planning on running the store for "another ten years or so." The couple names the disadvantages of owning the store as including the amount of time the work requires, and the fact that they haven't been able to travel, which they have always enjoyed doing. "During the summer, you see everybody else traveling and you just can't leave. But we love our business, so it works."

Social Marketing as a Career

Throughout this book, we stress the importance of having a solid plan before packing up and moving to paradise (see Chapter 6 for a ten-step plan for getting started). But there are exceptions to any rule. Charles Willard is proof that you don't necessarily need an elaborate business plan. You don't even need to know what kind of business you want to run once you get to paradise. What you do need, however, is a solid appreciation for your own strengths and weaknesses, some ingenuity, and the determination to succeed.

To anyone who asks about his vocation, Charles describes himself as a "professional socialite," and he says it in such a charming Texas drawl that he leaves you with no doubt of his sincerity. To be sure, "professional socialite" could mean any number of things, and any number of professions. To Charles Willard, being a professional socialite means that he has established his entrepreneurial career not by developing businesses, but by developing himself first, and funneling his skills into a social marketing career. His honest assessment about the skills he possesses—and his faith in relying on them—are the keys to the success of his small business in paradise.

Could You Pull Off a Consulting Business?

Think about something you love to do and research what you would need to do to make it a viable business. Do you enjoy following the stock market? Taking apart computers? Planning parties and other big, boisterous events? Writing persuasively? With these passions, you could become, respectively, a financial, computer, wedding, or marketing consultant. Type in the form of consulting you are interested in (such as "financial consulting") and the word "business" into your favorite search engine and find business plans and even professional associations for existing consultants in that field.

People seek paradise for different reasons. For some, like B&B owners Cecily Denson and Richard Pratt, it is to escape the rat race. For others like photographer Keoki Flagg, who is profiled in Chapter 5, it is a passion for his art. For individuals like Charles, dramatic life developments trigger the change, and two such life-altering events drove him to the Sonoma County hills.

Charles began his professional life in the army, leaving in 1969 to work for General Dynamics as a flight test engineer on F-111 aircraft. In the mid-1970s, he met an executive at retail conglomerate Carter Hawley Hale who convinced him that his people skills were being wasted, and that Charles should come to work for him as a merchandising executive. He climbed the corporate ladder for ten years, moving later to Federated Department Stores and then to become the national sales manager and director of marketing position at InterBath, a Los Angeles manufacturing company. The more he climbed the corporate ladder, the more he traveled for business, and the more he became estranged from his wife and two children. "I would be gone for 30 days at a time," he remembers. Then, one day, he returned home from a business trip to find the children at a relative's house, and his wife gone. The children, Mark and Amy, were three and five years old at the time, and Charles made the commitment to raise them on his own. "It made me rethink my career and my life," he says. So he began preparing for an eventual exit from his nine-to-five job at InterBath by accepting offers for part-time work as a marketing consultant. "People came to me because of the success I had. One of the products I helped introduce was the WaterPik shower massage. The packaging and the literature were very successful."

Soon after his entry into part-time work, a second life-altering event befell Charles. His daughter began having severe stomach cramps, and doctors blamed the Los Angeles air pollution. At the time—the late 1970s and early 1980s—clean air initiatives were yet to be implemented, and Los Angeles's air pollutant levels were off the charts. "She literally got the bends from playing too hard in the smog," he explains. As her illness became chronic, Charles knew the only solution was to get out of Los Angeles. So he packed up the kids, and just drove north. "We needed to drink fresh well water and breathe clean air." About an hour north of San Francisco, after passing miles of cattle-grazing land and farms near Petaluma, the little family crossed the Cotati Hills and "our breath was just taken away by the view. We picked a place to live on a hill in the little town of Penngrove, and things were better."

The Penngrove air was just the cure his daughter needed, but the environment was also a cure for Charles, relieving him of the stresses of city life and allowing him to focus on his career as a marketing consultant. Money wasn't a big concern at the time, and he had no shortage of potential clients from the relationships he had built in his previous careers.

He also discovered he could develop successful lines of business "just by getting out of the house and meeting people." For example, one colleague suggested he meet a friend who worked for a woodworking company in Petaluma. He did and both parties benefited from the meeting—Charles was engaged as marketing consultant, and he helped the company increase its sales. While he had marketed products for a long time, more and more he found he was marketing his own skills. Soon he was designing brochures and product packaging, putting together sales organizations and designing strategic marketing plans, mainly for manufacturing companies. Many of them were foreign companies seeking a U.S. presence, most of whom he met through referrals generated from his prior career in Los Angeles. To his delight, he was doing all of it from his own home. He also started an import-export business with a Chinese-American partner in San Francisco, who he had met while working for the state of California on a vehicle recovery program—an outgrowth of his work with various foreign companies. Soon they were shipping products all over the Pacific—animal feed, live chicks, food processing and manufacturing equipment, even cars.

Charles saw his children through grade school and then high school. After five years in Penngrove, he met and then married Patricia, who also had children from a previous marriage. She brought a mind for business, too, and soon she became his marketing assistant. They also bought several pieces of real estate over the years, and supplemented their income as landlords.

 FIND OUT MORE

For legal and tax rules that apply to consultants, check out *Working for Yourself: Law & Taxes for Independent Contractors, Freelancers & Consultants*, by Stephen Fishman (Nolo). This book explains how to choose the right business structure, set up home or outside offices, comply with IRS rules, avoid unfair contracts, draft good agreements, and get paid in full and on time.

The Willards found themselves doing more and more business in and around the towns of Sonoma, Glen Ellen, and Kenwood, 20 miles from Penngrove. "The drive from Penngrove across the hill toward Glen Ellen just speaks to my soul," Charles says. Indeed, the pastoral setting is reminiscent of California a century ago—plush green hills lined with vineyards, or populated with sheep, llamas, Nubian goats, and Black Angus cows. Then he was recruited to become the general manager of a food processing plant in Sonoma, and that was the final incentive the Willards needed to move again—this time to the town of Sonoma.

Like Penngrove, Sonoma was an idyllic setting to live in. However, where Penngrove was rural, quiet, and at times, isolated, Sonoma was bustling, with an old-world charm, enchanting town square, and Tuscany-like atmosphere. Sonoma was also a much better place to build Charles's business as a "professional socialite."

"Sonoma is an intriguing place," he says now. "There are so many talented people here—from retired business executives to writers, artists, actors, baseball players, and airline pilots. The other day I met Frank Sinatra's former gardener! They're everywhere you go. Even if they are retired, most of them continue working at something, and they are all involved in the community."

Making contact with interesting, gifted people, and recognizing and exploring opportunities when they become available, has been Charles's life in Sonoma since 1997. Today, he still works as a marketing consultant, still does import-export work, occasionally negotiates contracts or scouts a location for a food processing plant, and hires himself out as a sort of event host and social emcee. One day a week he pours wine in the tasting room at the Mayo Family Winery in Glen Ellen. And he does it all very well!

"Will Rogers said he had opinions on everything, but was an expert on nothing. That's me, I guess. And I like it that way. I never wanted a doctorate degree."

Charles proves that one can start a business in not just one, but two, paradise locations. However, it must have taken something more than a good personality. What was his secret? Perhaps two components of his success were his clear self-knowledge—he knew what skills he had to offer from prior careers—and his ability to pitch them to others. Charles also had the confidence to act on his beliefs about what he needed to do—whether it was moving out of Los Angeles, or going out to meet people. But it may be his genuine interest in people that is at the heart of his success.

"People just tell me things in the first five minutes after we've met that they wouldn't tell people they have known for five years. They just open up. It's not just an ability to listen, but an ability to empathize. You send out a signal that you're safe and it's okay to talk about yourself."

Charles also is willing to accept—and move on from—his mistakes. "Don't bring the past into the present," he says. "When things don't work out, don't brood on them. It's over and done. You have to give yourself permission to fail."

What now for Charles Willard? At the age of 61, he's thinking of retirement in the not-too-distant future. Of course, retirement to him won't be a condo in Sun City or shuffleboard on the cruise ship. Charles and Patricia are considering buying a home in Tuscany—his third paradise setting—where they can "retire for half the year" while still running their businesses. And who knows? Perhaps Charles's skills as a "professional socialite" will be in demand in Italy as well—that is, unless Italy already has enough of such characters!

Part-Time Paradise

Paradise doesn't have to be a full-time job. To some people, like Keith Savitz, owning a piece of paradise doesn't even require that you live there.

Keith is the quintessential Wall Street financial guy—a former vice president at Morgan Stanley, in 1999 he co-founded QUODD Financial, a provider of real-time market data to brokerage houses. He works long beyond the eight-hour day and admits that he "lives and breathes QUODD Financial." But Keith has something else in his life that keeps him going—he's the co-owner of the East End Café, a restaurant and bar in Red Hook, on the Caribbean island of St. Thomas.

"Everybody has to have a balance in their lives. The East End Café is my balance," Keith says. How he came to own the East End Café is a tale of spontaneity, "stick-to-itiveness," blind trust, and simply being in the right place at the right time.

Growing up, Keith's family often took family vacations to the Caribbean, and at one point owned a condo on St. Thomas in the Secret Harbour Beach Resort. During one trip in 1999, Keith went to a local surfer bar called "The Big Kahuna," a typical Caribbean beach bars with surfboards on the walls, pool tables, and people in shorts, with sand and seawater dripping onto the floors. There he met Zach Zoller, a local who owned the Big Kahuna with two other partners. Zach and Keith quickly struck up a friendship, and soon Zach was telling him how one of the three partners wasn't working out. Seeing an opportunity, Keith approached the partner, and found that he too wanted out of his investment. Within two weeks after meeting Zach, Keith had signed a check to purchase a third of the Big Kahuna. "My family and friends thought I was crazy to write these guys a check two weeks after I met them. But sometimes you have to go with your gut, and I had a gut feeling that I could trust them."

Now Zach, Keith, and third owner Jeff Kromenhoek, also a local resident, "are like brothers." The Big Kahuna has been renamed the East End Café, specializes in Italian cuisine and seafood, and attracts a more upscale crowd of both locals and tourists. Investment in several remodeling projects have gradually transformed the restaurant into a pleasant place for both lunch and dinner, as well as an appealing locale for late-night cocktails. Their future plans include adding a wine bar and meeting place that will remain open until 2 or 3 a.m., long after the restaurant area shuts down.

Keith's role in the restaurant is that of a silent partner. He leaves all the management of the East End Café to Zach and Jeff. "You'd think he was the mayor," Keith says of Zach, who has been instrumental in forming partnerships with other local business owners and establishing the East End as a gathering place for locals, in addition to a destination spot for tourists. As most owners of businesses in paradise discover, local residents are crucial in keeping the restaurant going during the slower months, which in St. Thomas is the period from April through November. (For more about the importance of establishing a community presence, see Chapter 11.)

Keith had neither the time nor the desire to build a restaurant and bar himself, and he didn't want to live on St. Thomas full-time. Like many people, however, the idea of owning a bar/restaurant in the Caribbean had always appealed to him. "You can start it from scratch. Or, like any business, you can come into it later—when someone else has already taken on some of the risk, and the business looks potentially prosperous."

Keith said he invested in the business after he realized how the Big Kahuna could be transformed and made more profitable. While remodeling costs have been considerable, they are not close to what it would have cost to have created an entirely new business.

Currently, Keith does not receive any dividends from the restaurant—profits are plowed back into the business. Without disclosing details, however, he says his share of the business is worth significantly more than it was when he bought it eight years ago, and he's already turned down several offers to purchase his ownership portion from other local entrepreneurs.

 FIND OUT MORE

Looking for Caribbean businesses for sale? Check out www. resortpathways.com/buying-a-resort.htm.

Keith visits the East End Café about three times a year, spending a week or a long weekend, and often staying with Zach or Jeff. "It's nice to be able to go down to St. Thomas a few times a year. The residents treat me like a local. Now, because of the restaurant and bar, I am friends with so many other people down there."

Keith also enjoys thinking about the naysayers who thought he was crazy, all of whom are now congratulating him on the success of the business. Many of them are even envious, especially when Keith takes them with him to St. Thomas, "and Jeff and Zach roll out the red carpet."

Although Keith's investment is not bringing in cash dividends, he has taken pleasure in seeing it become successful, and it has filled the void he needed it to fill—that need for balance to his life on Wall Street. "Plus, it takes zero time on my part. I just bought it. Jeff and Zach do all the work. And when you're sitting near the beach, drinking cocktails in the Caribbean at your own bar and restaurant, there's no better place to be."

Tips for Would-Be Entrepreneurs

What lessons can the experiences of this group of businesspeople offer? If you find yourself considering an opportunity for business in paradise, consider the following:

Understand the Risks

Every small business in paradise comes with a certain amount of risk. The key is understanding the level of risk involved, and to make sure you're comfortable with it. For Fiona and David, buying Candy & Kites was clearly a big, life-altering step, so they took their time, testing the waters by working in the store for six months before buying. For Keith Savitz, buying a share of The Big Kahuna was an extremely risky investment, but he wasn't committing himself and his time to the venture—only his money—and it was an amount of money he could afford to lose. Keith's advice about restaurants is really apt for all small businesses in paradise: "Don't go into it unless you understand it's a tremendous amount of risk, and you know you'd be all right if you lost your entire investment. Go into it knowing that, and with a passion for what you're doing. And have fun."

Just Any Paradise Won't Do

Choosing locations is discussed more in Chapter 7 but it's worth pointing out here how different businesses do well in different settings. The Big Kahuna did well as a surf bar, but as its owners, its customers and the community of Red Hook all matured, the more sophisticated East End Café was more appropriate for its clientele (and consequently more successful than a beach bar). A store selling candy and kites can do well on the coast at Bodega Bay, where there's plenty of wind, a steady stream of tourists, and little competition. And a career in social marketing will likely be more successful in a town like Sonoma than in other less-networked communities where the arts and charitable events are not such an important component of the business community. Sonoma, although rural, is prosperous, and its industries—wine, hospitality, restaurants—assign a value to people who conduct themselves well socially.

Only You Will Know When an Opportunity Is Right

If you frequent a paradise location, opportunities for work and businesses will eventually present themselves. While it may be tempting to jump at every opportunity, be sure the choices you make are consistent with the life you want. As Charles summarized: "Opportunities come, but you often have so many that you need to be selective as to where you put your energies and time. Otherwise, you are not focused enough on your end goals." Likewise, you ultimately must decide what is a good move for you, even if others disagree. To his friends, it seemed that Keith Savitz was taking a huge risk, but he wouldn't have done so if he didn't recognize the opportunity as being right for him. If he had passed it up, he may have regretted it and, with that in mind, might have later settled for a business with less potential or partners in whom he had less trust.

Get Out and Meet People

If you are considering a business opportunity, the best way to know whether you will like being there is to meet others in the community. Are there like-minded people who you see yourself having over for dinner? Are the local residents open to new faces? (See "Scout the Territory" in Chapter 6 for more about investigating whether a community is right for you.) In addition to getting a sense of your comfort level in the paradise location, the success of any business you own is dependent on getting to know the people in the community. Most paradise locations are set in regions with small populations, and word about any topic spreads quickly among the residents. Here, perhaps more than in larger communities, relationship-building is a key component of business success. For David, Fiona, and Keith, focusing on establishing personal relationships has not only built their clientele, but provided the opportunity to get involved in their businesses in the first place. For Charles, whose business can ostensibly be run from home with a computer, fax machine, and cell phone, there is no substitute for face-to-face contact. He views personal contact as necessary both to get a deal moving or a relationship established, and also important toward the end of a transaction, when a final meeting is more likely to result in additional work or perhaps referrals for new business. See Chapter 11 for more about the need for small business owners to become acquainted with, and participate, in the community.

Taking Passion to Paradise

Passion and paradise seem to mix well, as evidenced by the abundance of people in paradise locations who are devoted to so-called "creative" professions—art, design, photography, gourmet cooking, writing, and the like. There's no way to teach passion for your work, but it is easily recognizable—you see it in the care and creativity which has gone into an art gallery show, taste it in the perfectly blended ingredients of a gourmet olive oil, and feel it when an artist enthusiastically describes his or her work.

The link between paradise locations and businesses stemming from a passionate pursuit—whether the arts or another pastime—may be explained in several ways. Creative individuals may be drawn to paradise because it inspires them. A painter looks over a crystal blue mountain lake and is compelled to recreate it on canvas; a sculptor sees the mastery of nature's rock formations and waterfalls, and is challenged to capture that grace in another medium. Another possibility is that the quietness and natural beauty associated with paradise locations frees the creative flow—if one isn't being hectored by the noise, traffic, and high cost of living of a densely populated area, presumably one can better focus on a creative pursuit. Additionally, paradise locations may attract different customers than in the city, or ones who are more relaxed and appreciative of what is offered. Someone on vacation may be more likely to visit a gallery or try a new sport than in his or her workaday world. While "passion" businesses can be located anywhere, any location in paradise is likely to support one or more.

Do you feel passionate about a particular craft or skill? Could you see yourself turning your passion into a viable business in paradise? This chapter profiles four business owners who have succeeded in turning their passions for art or a hobby into successful small businesses.

Ginger and Her Garden of Eden

Just off the Kuhio Highway south of Kapaa on the island of Kauai, tucked into the edge of an old sugar plantation, is an idyllic little garden restaurant called Caffe Coco. Ginger Carlson, the 60-year-old owner of Caffe Coco, usually starts her day negotiating with local fishermen. After careful inspection, she will buy several fish that will become part of her unique recipes—perhaps including a pineapple glaze or a coconut milk sauce—and be served up later that day on the plates of her customers.

It's easy to miss Caffe Coco unless you know where to look, but word of mouth has been good to Ginger, and even in the off season, the place fills up at night. No customer is disappointed. The atmosphere of the restaurant exudes the passion of the owner for her work. "Casual elegance" is how Ginger describes that atmosphere, but the phrase does not capture the feel of the well-appointed, garden-style dining area, situated under a tropical canopy of orchids, jasmine, palm trees, bamboo, and passion fruit. Broken pieces of Italian ceramic pottery are embedded into the floor, the tables, and the lamps—all remnants of Ginger's pottery collection which was destroyed—along with her house—in California's 1989 Loma Prieta earthquake. The lighting is soft and mostly natural— the tiny flames of tiki torches bounce in the island breeze. But the food—a mélange of southern Italian style, tropical island ingredients, and Ginger's creativity—is the main reason people come here. Ginger's food is known for its healthy orientation, and includes no red meat or trans fats. The organic salads and tofu potstickers come highly recommended, as does her signature Ginger Lemonade.

A SMALL BUSINESS IN *Paradise*

If these dishes sound good to you, read more of Caffe Coco's menu at www.restauranteur.com/caffecoco/index.htm.

The restaurant is a fusion of all of Ginger's passions—Italian cooking, Hawaii, gardening, Italian ceramics. While Ginger insists there's a spiritual source underlying her success, it's also clear that her own flair for business and her prior successes have helped make Caffe Coco what it is today.

FIND OUT MORE

For a directory covering every issue the aspiring restaurateur could want to know, try www.allfoodbusiness.com. From writing a business plan to lighting design to a glossary of terms, this site will point you in the most delicious directions.

Ginger's first job in the restaurant business was as a waitress in St. Louis. However, she quickly discovered that she preferred preparing food to serving it, and went to work in the kitchen. There she found her calling as a chef, and in her early twenties was working as a caterer to many of St. Louis's top families, including the Pulitzers. By age 25, she opened her first restaurant, Duff's, with a partner, and ran it for ten years. Having made Duff's a success, she sold her share for a substantial profit and moved to Stevensville, Michigan, where she bought Tosi's—a 47-year-old Italian restaurant. At Tosi's, Ginger made her mark as a restaurateur, transforming it into one of Michigan's top restaurants and gaining national recognition. She was so intent on offering authentic Italian meals at the eatery that she took 21 members of her staff to Italy for a two-and-a-half week tour of restaurants and wineries. She later added another restaurant, Caffe Tosi, just five miles away.

In 1989, however, tragedy struck. Ginger's son and only child was diagnosed with a fatal form of anemia. She quickly sold her share in the Tosi's restaurants and moved to California in search of alternative healing methods, while simultaneously embarking on a new career as a restaurant consultant. Within one year after moving, Ginger and her husband divorced, their son died, her father passed away, and the earthquake struck. "There I was at the lowest point of my life, and I got a call from someone in Kauai who wanted me to help them open a health food restaurant."

"I just became enthralled with Kauai," she recalls. After completing the consulting job, she went back to California, packed up her things, lined up another consulting job in Kauai, and moved there for good in 1991. With the proceeds from the sale of Tosi's still lining her pockets, money wasn't an immediate concern, so she took five years off from the restaurant business to paint, garden, read travel books, and create her own line of Kauai-based products—chutneys, jams, salad dressings, and grilling sauces made from local ingredients such as guavas and pineapple.

Dreaming of Palm Trees?

Apparently you are not alone. The Aloha State offers practical advice on its website about relocating to Hawaii and starting your own business. Visit www.hawaii.gov/dbedt/business/start_grow.

"After five years, I wanted to give something back to Kauai—to do something that was about freedom and meaning, instead of just to earn a living. So I meditated on what to do next. And the answer that came to me was that I was supposed to open another restaurant. I had the sense that it was going to be a special restaurant. And people would come from all over the world and appreciate the level of care and consideration for the way I prepare food."

And so, Caffe Coco was born.

Sometimes an entrepreneur's passion and vision can clash with bureaucracy, and that was the case with Ginger. Her vision of an open-air restaurant in a natural setting, with no exhaust fans and no fluorescent lighting, ran counter to several county codes. "I wanted visitors to feel as if they were coming to my home and eating in my backyard." She built the restaurant the way she wanted to, and suffered the consequences of bucking county bureaucracy by paying some fines. In the end, however, the necessary permits were issued, and her restaurant was allowed to operate in its quirky format.

Caffe Coco celebrated its ten-year anniversary in 2007, and is now a local landmark and a profitable venture for Ginger. Nevertheless, even with her extensive experience in restaurant management, Caffe Coco has been a struggle. Years of renovations to the old sugar shacks that became Caffe Coco were exhausting—physically, emotionally, and financially. Winning the support of local officials and local customers has also been daunting. "I'm still considered an outsider," she says. Seasonal swings make it difficult to manage the business at times, and an overall drop in tourism since the terrorist attacks of September 11, 2001, have hurt Ginger's business and the local economy. Managing her workforce has been another challenge. She trained chefs to take over when she's not there, but Hawaii law requires that employers pay health care and other benefits to anyone who works more than 19 hours a week. Because of the prohibitive cost of full-time employees, Caffe Coco—like many Hawaiian businesses—employs many part-time workers who also work two or three other jobs.

Because of these continuing challenges, Ginger has decided to leave the restaurant business again—this time for good, she says. Caffe Coco is for sale. "Someone very lucky is going to get it. But I won't sell it if they're going to turn it into a pizzeria."

Like many entrepreneurs, though, Ginger's "retirement" will be an active one. She lives on a seven-acre estate, and she plans to turn it into a nursery, once again putting her passion to work. She has named the nursery "The Ginger Grove." While she'll continue to sell the jams and jellies she has produced almost since moving to Kauai, she will also expand her catering business. In running the restaurant, she's found a catering business niche, serving Hollywood film crews working on the island. At the time of her interview, she was working on the set of *Tropic Thunder*, a DreamWorks film starring Ben Stiller.

"I do consider this my final chapter, and it's going to be a nice long one." With running three businesses, it sounds like it will be busy as well.

FIND OUT MORE

Becoming a caterer is a great way to work for yourself in the food industry, but without the overhead of a dining room. Not needing customer facilities keeps costs low, and allows you maximum time with the star of the show: the food. *How to Start a Home-Based Catering Business,* by Denise Vivaldo (Globe Pequot), is an excellent resource for a foodie with a kitchen calling.

A Board, a Wave, a Surf Shop

You have to be hard-core to surf regularly in Bodega Bay. The water and air are cold, the weather is often cloudy, and the best surfing spots are the rocky shorelines north of town, near Salmon Creek, where 12-foot swells can punish even the most skilled surfers. Bodega Bay, best known as the setting for Alfred Hitchcock's *The Birds,* is also the home of Robert Miller, better known by almost everyone in town as Surfer Bob.

Bob is the owner of the Bodega Bay Surf Shack—a small retail store in a tiny shopping center just a stone's throw from the ocean. Anyone who surfs in Bodega knows Bob. He sells surfing gear, rents boards and wetsuits, gives surf lessons, and can usually tell you on any given day what the local surfing conditions are, including where the best waves can be found. Bob's passion for surfing borders on obsession. At 40, he's always tan and still speaks with a surfer accent reminiscent of Sean Penn's Jeff Spicoli character in *Fast Times at Ridgemont High.* He has traveled the world to surf—Australia, Fiji, Indonesia, Hawaii—and still hits the waves practically every day, often twice a day.

Bob's career path has been very focused, and can be described as the pursuit of ways to live and breathe surfing: "If I can't be on the waves 24 hours a day, at least I can do the next best thing: work at a surf shack."

Bob began surfing in the 1980s, while attending high school in Santa Rosa, California. At the time, he was working at a pizza restaurant. "It was the last time I ever worked for 'the man,'" Bob recalls. In the late

A SMALL BUSINESS
IN
Paradise

To find out more about The Surf Shack, see http://bodegabaysurf.com.

1980s, he got a job at a surf shop in nearby Sebastopol. "I just felt so lucky that I could do what I wanted to do, and get paid for it."

The owner of the Sebastopol shop later opened a shop in Bodega Bay, and asked Bob to work there. Seeing an opportunity to be even closer to the ocean, Bob quickly

agreed. Soon Bob was living out of the trunk of his car and the shop, while surfing for hours every day. By 1993, Bob had saved up enough money to buy the shop: "I lived simply—totally roughing it. There were some sacrifices. I started a window-cleaning service on the side. I took everything I made and put it back into the shop."

A typical day for Bob began at dawn, when he would climb out of his car/bedroom, brush his teeth at the surf shop, spend a couple of hours cleaning windows, then hit the waves and surf for another couple of hours, finishing in time to open the shop at 10 a.m.

The lease for the shop, $1,500 a month when he bought the business, was more than he could afford, so he looked around for a less expensive space. He eventually found a tiny little space in a shopping center near the beach for $500 a month. At 300 square feet, it was a quarter the size of the other space. But with true ingenuity, Bob created a system of hooks, pulleys, and ropes and crammed all of the gear from the larger place into the new Bodega Bay Surf Shack. Surfboards are suspended from the ceilings, and every inch of wall space is covered with shirt racks, sunglasses, wetsuits, and other gear.

Twelve years later, the Bodega Bay Surf Shop is going strong and has become a fixture in the small town, just like Bob. He's been married for ten years to Lauri, a fellow surfer who Bob describes as "just as radical as I am. Lauri isn't into the surf shack, but she's a great surfer. She's always been my sidekick, and I couldn't have done it without her." They have two sons, Miles, eight years old, and Dylan, three.

 FIND OUT MORE

For the world's top surf spots or anything surf-related, check out www.surfline.com.

With the surf shack now making a steady profit, Bob recently opened a second business, Bodega Bay Kayak. He and Lauri also own a rental property about 25 miles up the coast. And he still gives surf lessons most days.

Bob's story is clearly one of following your passion at all costs. His never-look-back attitude, ability to make sacrifices, and patience have all paid off in the long run, with a comfortable income, a home near the water, and a job that allows him to keep surfing every day. "I just feel so blessed," he says.

Japanese Art—In a California Fishing Village?

Bodega Bay is above all a fishing village, so Surfer Bob was an anomaly for a long time. But even Surfer Bob doesn't seem as out of place as the Ren Brown Gallery—a facility with decor as beautifully precise as the Japanese art it displays, and a stunning Japanese garden out back. Somehow, it works. In fact, the Ren Brown gallery seems to highlight the serenity and natural beauty of Bodega Bay, providing a reminder of what the area was like before being populated by humans.

Ren Brown was a nurse by trade. In 1989, he was working at a children's hospital in Oakland and living in Berkeley with his partner, Robert, an artist. As Ren recalls, "One evening after one glass of wine too many, Robert said, 'Why don't we move to the Sonoma Coast?' I agreed."

"There was no pediatric hospital in Sonoma County, and I needed an occupation. So, I thought about turning my hobby into a business." Ren had been collecting Japanese art since high school, when he and his family spent several years living in Japan. However, neither he nor Robert had any experience running a business of any kind, including an art gallery.

"The thing we had going for us was our complete faith that this might work," Ren recalls.

Their first step was to start calling realtors, but soon found how challenging it would be to find a place where they could both live and work, which meant that the property would need to be zoned for both commercial and residential purposes. After several months of searching, they finally found a parcel of land with a building on the west (or ocean) side of Highway 1, the scenic highway running down the middle of Bodega Bay. The two-story building

A SMALL BUSINESS IN Paradise

Visit the Ren Brown Gallery online at www.renbrown.com.

had a small apartment upstairs, and an unfinished garage downstairs that had potential as a gallery space, and was zoned for commercial use. Even better, an adjoining parcel of land—with a house on it—was also for sale.

"We had to completely remodel the gallery building. Luckily, we had good friends who were architects, so they drew up the plans. And we hired contractors to do the work." The remodel took eight or nine months to complete. As completion neared, a field of weeds in front of the building was turned into a crushed gravel parking lot, and soon thereafter, the Ren Brown Gallery was in business.

Two early business decisions served Ren and Robert well. First, before moving to Bodega, Ren started attending art shows and marketing himself as a dealer of Japanese art. As a collector, he already had ties with several Japanese artists, most of them living in Japan, so he developed those relationships further and soon had inventory for the gallery. Second, they bought the gallery building and their home outright for cash, so they weren't encumbered by lease or mortgage payments. As a backup plan, they planned to rent out the gallery space if the business didn't work out. (See Chapter 6 for more about creating exit plans when starting a business.)

As Ren recalls: "Our friends thought we were crazy to try selling Japanese art in this small fishing village in the boondocks. But we had a few things going for us. We figured the advantage of doing business here is that you're a big fish in a small pond. There are not too many options here for things to do and places to see. If someone visits Bodega Bay for a weekend, they are most likely going to find us."

The gallery also served as a place to display Robert's art, along with the work of several other local artists that, per Ren, "fit into the purview of the gallery." In addition, the gallery offers Japanese antiques and gift items so customers may find items they like in a range of prices.

Like Fiona and David of Candy & Kites, profiled in Chapter 4, Ren discovered early on that his experience in a service industry—in his case, hospitals—would come in handy in the gallery. As a nurse, helping people and making them feel comfortable were essential skills. In an art gallery, he explains, "You need to offer assistance to people without getting in the way of them finding what they want. Many people don't feel confident about their artistic opinions. Even smart, savvy people sometimes feel on shaky ground when they are looking at art, especially that of a culture so different from their own. Our approach is to make the environment comforting, supportive, and relaxed. If we can educate our customers in a nonthreatening environment, they are more likely to return."

While customer service came easy, other aspects of owning and managing a small business presented more of a challenge to Ren: "I had to learn about advertising and writing press releases, picture framing, and some accounting. It is amazing to realize how much you don't know about running a business when you jump in feet first. Issues always come up you aren't prepared to handle. Dealing with employees is another area of worry for any small business owner. Employee issues can be a big headache, because no one is going to care about your business as much as you do." (See Chapter 9 for further discussion on meeting the challenges of being an employer.)

While Ren had to learn many business skills on the fly, he stuck with it. He is now 60 years old. Robert, 67, has Parkinson's disease and hasn't been painting as much as he used to do. But the gallery is thriving, and Ren says they have no plans to either move, change, or grow the business. "We support ourselves. And we keep buying more inventory," he smiles, "so I guess we're doing okay."

If Ren sees a downside to their move, it's that Bodega Bay is far from the culturally rich, cosmopolitan areas of San Francisco and Berkeley that Ren called home for years. "I miss being able to go to an Ethiopian restaurant. There is no opera, no ballet, seldom a symphony, and the nearest bookstore is half an hour away. But it is politically liberal here, which is good for us, and socially accepting to gay people. And the sound of the waves when you are going to sleep just can't be beat. Besides, it is hugely satisfying to carve out your own niche, to make something out of nothing—especially when all your friends thought you couldn't do it."

A Photographer's Passion

Keoki Flagg is a world-renowned adventure photographer. His photos have graced magazines such as *Ski, Skiing, National Geographic Adventure, Men's Journal, Vogue, Audubon,* and *Outside.* Some of them, including a humorous shot of golden retrievers on a ski lift, have been splashed across multiple media and are familiar to thousands of people.

Found hanging at ski lodges, coffee shops, and sporting goods shops, his photographs are often of people on skis or snowboards, performing extreme feats in some of the most beautiful places in the world. They're the kind of photos that make you wonder, "How the hell did he take that picture?"

FIND OUT MORE

If you're going to pursue photography as a career, the mandatory first stop on your business venture is *The Photographer's Market* (Writers Digest), updated yearly and now in its 30th edition.

That quest for purity compelled Keoki to open Gallery Keoki in 2003. The gallery is located in the village at Squaw Valley, near Lake Tahoe, California. "The reason the gallery is so important to me is that I can control what is best about my work," Keoki says, who at the time of his interview, had just returned from a photo shoot in Alaska with extreme sports filmmaker Warren Miller. "The most important reason for the gallery, the ultimate goal, is to remove economics from my art."

A SMALL BUSINESS IN *Paradise*

If you would like to learn more about Keoki's business, visit www.gallerykeoki.com.

Keoki has been an artist all his life. Born and raised primarily in Hawaii, his adventurous parents also took him to live in Spain, Switzerland, and France when he was young, and on camping trips that lasted months at a time. "When I was 18, I already knew what else the world had to offer, and I wanted off 'the rock' (the islands of Hawaii)." He studied art and history at Connecticut College, a small liberal arts school. For a time, sculpture was his greatest passion. He painted houses to earn extra cash in college, and when he graduated, bought a house-painting franchise that he managed for two years. "That experience gave me the confidence that I could make a living. It also gave me enough cash to pay off my college debt and to travel. I felt accomplished as an artist coming out of school, but I didn't have enough life experiences." So Keoki took two trips, each two years in length—the first to New Zealand, Australia, and Southeast Asia, the second to other parts of Asia and Africa. The more he traveled, the more he put his passion into photography, in part because sculpting wasn't practical while on the move, and in part because he found he could make a living by selling his photos to magazines. "I was very spontaneous and very free, and I moved around a lot," he recalls. In between his trips, he stayed with his parents for several months at their new home near Lake Tahoe, and per Keoki, "just fell in love with the place."

A year after returning from his second trip, Keoki staged his first art show—a collection of photos of people in Third World countries—at a small Lake Tahoe gallery. "I put the show together myself, doing the printing, production, and framing, and I realized then that that was how I wanted to sell my photography." The show was a success, and led to another show, and another. Magazine work still paid most of his bills, however, and he found he had to take magazine jobs to cover his living expenses and buy the photographic gear and supplies he needed. "Somewhere along the way, photography became a job," he said. He pointed to a photo of himself traveling in the Third World, wearing nothing but shorts and sandals and standing next to a native half his size. "I lost the balance I had when I was that guy."

 FIND OUT MORE

If you're a creative type, and want to use these skills to financial advantage, try *Start & Run A Creative Services Business*, by Susan Kirkland (Self-Counsel Press). A veteran freelancer, Kirkland gives real-world advice that will be useful to anyone beginning a creative business venture.

Keoki realized he needed to take a different direction with his art, and decided to open a gallery. He started small, with his own combination gallery and studio in Tahoe City, but then his father introduced him to Mark Steingard, an international art dealer who, by chance, was in his father's hiking group. The two struck up a friendship, developing a mutual respect for each other. Two years later, Intrawest ULC, the developers of the Village at Squaw Valley (an alpine-style shopping center at the base of the resort), proposed that Keoki open a gallery in the village. While intrigued, Keoki did not personally have the funds needed to participate in the deal, so he wrote Mark asking what he thought of the venture. Mark also saw the potential and the two formed a partnership, deciding to open a gallery that would show Keoki's work alongside international masters such as Miró and Picasso. The partnership was a challenge right from the start because each of them had different opinions about the direction of the business, and both had strong personalities. Nevertheless, Keoki accepted Mark's authority due to the latter's business experience and natural management skills: "I had to decide that there was nothing more important than this gallery, and I agreed to play a supportive role in its operation."

Consequently, for the first three years, Mark made most of the business decisions, drawing on his expertise to build the gallery into a thriving business and one of the Tahoe area's most reputable galleries. The partners recognized that their clients typically fell into one of three groups, two of which were tourists looking for one or two pieces to take home to adorn their walls, and local residents who appreciate art and have the means to buy it. The group of clients responsible for the greatest portion of the gallery's revenue, however, were the vacation home owners, many of whom lived in the San Francisco Bay Area and spent weekends and vacations in Tahoe. Of this group, many would buy not just one or two paintings and/or photos, but enough pieces to ornament their entire cabin. (Keep in mind that the word "cabin" in Tahoe may refer to a ten-room pine mansion with vaulted ceilings and a stunning view.)

In his work at the gallery, Keoki was not only selling his own photos, but also helping his clients stage them and other artists' works in their homes and businesses. Meanwhile, showing his work in the gallery helped increase the interest in, and value of, his own work. "It doesn't hurt when your photo is hanging next to a Picasso," he laughs.

Mark implemented most of the gallery's business practices, which include a 30-day return policy, and a right to trade in any piece of investment art (typically originals by well-known artists) for five years following its purchase from the gallery. The rationale for the latter policy is that investment-grade art tends to increase in value anywhere from 10% to 25% a year, so if a client wants to return something a few years after they buy it, the gallery not only keeps its clients happy, but can also profit from buying a work back for its original price and reselling it at a higher price.

Marketing for the gallery has been largely dependent on Keoki and the relationships he has developed over his years in the Tahoe area. The gallery currently lends Keoki's work to 22 other businesses around the region. These other businesses—shops, hotel lobbies, and restaurants—showcase Keoki's work (and market the gallery) while gracing their own walls with world-class photography. Similarly, Keoki lets local magazines and newspapers (which typically have small budgets for photography) use his photos in exchange for advertising space for his gallery.

"The barter system is alive and well in resorts and small towns," Keoki says. "There are a lot of entrepreneurial people here who are struggling, and are willing to help each other get ahead." (See "Hello Big Brother," below.) He also barters with ski resorts—lending them photos to hang in their lodges, in return for free ski passes for his employees—and with sporting goods makers, featuring their gear in his photos in exchange for equipment for himself and his staff. The result is not only an efficient way to market his photos and reduce his costs, but a community-building exercise that builds the gallery's reputation and fuels referrals. "Getting this gallery off the ground was a true test of the support I have in the community. Every time I hit a wall or an obstacle, somebody stepped up and solved it for me."

Hello Big Brother

Note that barter income—or what you or your business receives in a noncash transaction—is usually reportable as income to the IRS. Go to www.irs.gov and type "barter" in the search box for more information about reporting requirements.

At some point over the past year, however, Keoki began to feel that the gallery was taking up too much of his time, and taking him away from his first passion—photography. While it may sound counterintuitive, the solution he came up with was to gradually take over the management of the gallery from his partner Mark, with the intention of building a team whose members could move into full-time management roles, allowing Keoki to spend more time away from the gallery. In Keoki's mind, the business needed to change the way the business recruited and retained employees: "It was clear to me that we were going to need a new management style if we were going to keep employees long-term." For instance, as a manager, Mark was more hands-on, and consequently didn't mind hiring less experienced people he could train. Keoki, on the other hand, whose goal is to spend less time at the gallery, is looking to hire experienced people with whom he could trust some of the management of the business.

Since the gallery was established and had a sizable base of return clients, Mark, who now spends a large part of the year in Florida and Arizona, was happy to relinquish the day-to-day management to Keoki. "I am now in control of the business," Keoki says. "Hopefully I will also regain control of my life as an artist. I realized that the only way to do that was to build a solid team to run the gallery when I'm not there." Keoki expects to continue working in the gallery during the peak seasons, and make use of the Tahoe "shoulder seasons"—May and June, and October and November—to take long jaunts in search of the photographic purity he seeks. "The magic moments that define my career will be those when I make that extra bit of effort—when I put on a harness and rappel an extra hundred yards to get that perfect shot." That extra bit of effort has paid off—both in the art of his photography, and in creating a business that supports his passion.

Passion Into Paradise: Key Points

If there's one lesson to learn from the stories of Ginger, Bob, Ren, and Keoki, it's that there is no single recipe for turning a passion into a viable business in paradise. However, all four of them were willing to do the following to make their ventures a success:

Trust the Creative Instinct

One overwhelming advantage that creative people have in starting a business is their creativity. Often "left-brained" or creative people are assumed to be at a loss when running a business, but that's not necessarily the case. Ginger's creativity has shown up not only in the variety of businesses she has started, but also in every aspect of her work, which has included transforming a sugar plantation shack into a restaurant and finding a way to fuse her passions for Italian food, Kauian ingredients, and a tropical atmosphere. Keoki came up with creative bartering techniques to get exposure for his gallery. Bob used his creativity to fit his boards and gear into a tiny rental space, and Ren created a Japanese garden to welcome guests to his gallery. By putting their creativity to use, all of these owners have distinguished their businesses from their competition, which has contributed to their success.

Cultivate Business Skills

Rarely does one person have all the skills necessary to make a business a success. Recognizing the ones you have, and the ones you need to attain—either through hiring or partnering with someone else or learning them yourself—is the first step to making your business work for you. As you will see from the remainder of the book, key business skills include, among others, understanding finance (making sure you know how your business can operate profitably), client relations (knowing how to develop and maintain a customer base), sales and marketing (knowing how to get customers to your business and sell them what you are offering), human resources management (how best to staff your business), and at least a rudimentary understanding of some of the legal issues you will face as a business owner. While this may seem like a daunting list, it's a myth that a creative person can't develop business acumen. You can partner with someone who brings those skills to the table, like Keoki did with Mark Steingard, or you can develop them yourself, like Ginger and Ren did. You may decide to take a course in small business management, or read more books about small business to further your learning. Know that many successful business owners didn't know a thing about business when getting started, and like Ren, learned on the job. You may even discover that you enjoy it, or that it provides a "right-brain" balance to your creative pursuits.

Separate the Craft From the Business

Starting a business based on your passion is not the same as pursuing the passion itself. There's no getting around the fact that the moment you start a business, the time you have available for the creative aspect of your profession will decrease. However, if you can look at the business as the "next best thing" to actually pursuing your art or hobby, like Bob the Surfer did, or as an interesting way to support your interest, you will more likely enjoy building a business. If not, you may feel frustrated, and business in paradise will instead feel like a trap. What you may also discover, as other small business owners have, is that running a business is itself an art, and, like Ren and Bob you may find you enjoy it. Further, if you manage the business well, and develop a staff you trust, you may be able take a step back from the day-to-day management and spend more time on your passions, as Keoki is trying to do. Alternatively, you may decide to leave the business in order to pursue the next passion, as Ginger is planning.

Know Your "One Thing"

Remember the Curly character (a leathery cowboy played by Jack Palance) from the movie *City Slickers*? When the Billy Crystal character asked about his life philosophy, Curly explained that it all came down to "one thing." That one thing varies from person to person. If like Bob the Surfer, you live and breathe one thing passionately, a small business may be the way for you to incorporate your passion into your livelihood. Knowing your vision, and keeping sight of it, then makes all decisions easier—either the step you are considering will further your goal or it will not. You may decide that a small business can provide a means to express your passion, develop it, and turn it into a career, even though taking that step can impact the rest of your life, and be a financial struggle as well. Or you may determine that starting a business will require you to give up your passion, at least for a while, just to make the business work. Either way, make the decision based on what will best serve your "one thing." If you decide to try a small business, read on. In the rest of this book, you'll find practical guidance and business tips that might make the journey a little more predictable, and the end result more fruitful. ●

Turn Your Dream Into Reality: Ten Steps for Getting Started

A s the profiles in Chapters 2 through 5 illustrate, each business owner follows a distinct path in establishing his or her business, complete with unique trials and challenges. If you are interested in starting your own small business in paradise, you will need to plot your own course. However, some of the questions to consider and tasks to accomplish are the same, regardless of your personal situation or the type of business you are considering. Follow the next ten steps (described more fully throughout this chapter) to think through the concept of your business, anticipate your challenges, and develop your own plan of action for addressing them:

1. Make sure the business fits you, and you fit the business. Will it hold your interest for years to come? Do you have the right skills set and personality? Are there classes you can take or information on the Internet that will help you understand the industry?

2. Check with those closest to you. Make sure that those most affected by your desire to pull up roots and set up shop (and life) elsewhere are included in your decision. Is there a place for them in the plan?

3. Scout the territory. Take at least two scouting trips to your planned destination—one during the peak season and one during the off-season. How would it feel to live there all year around?

4. Gauge market demand and check out the competition. Is there a market for your goods and services in the area? Can the community support another dentist office, for instance?

5. Estimate your startup costs. How much will it take to get your business off the ground?

6. Do a break-even analysis. How much income will you need to bring in to cover your costs every month?

7. Write a business plan—really. Where are you going with the business and how are you going to get there?

8. Put together your business financing. How will you fund your start-up costs and your growth?

9. Have a "Plan B." What will you do if your business in paradise turns out to be a bust, or if you do not like the work?

10. Get your current house in order. How easily can you wrap up your business dealings where you now live and work?

Granted, that is a long list of things to do. However, thinking through the details of a dream business will help illuminate whether your quality of life will be improved by the change—or if it is unlikely to work and may create hardship. (Additionally, this chapter and the rest of the book will offer resources for accomplishing many of these tasks.) As you investigate the possibilities, you may also discover an alternate path that works better for you than the one you originally considered. Whatever the result, your work is fruitful in that you have determined the best course of action for you (and your family, if you have one). Now let's take a closer look at each of the ten steps.

Make Sure the Business Fits You, and You Fit the Business

When deciding whether a business fits you, ask yourself whether it will hold your interest for years to come, and matches the lifestyle you want. If you are very interested in art and would like to open a gallery, are you prepared to run a retail establishment, requiring you to be present at certain hours and on certain days? Conversely, making sure you fit the business requires an honest look at your skills set and personality—you may love fly fishing, be really good at it, and dream of your own fly-fishing shop. But have you had experience working with suppliers and managing inventory? Are you good with people and able to manage both customer relationships and employees? Do you have the entrepreneurial qualities needed to start and manage a business? All these are necessary if you're planning to make your store a success.

Before embarking on your journey to paradise, take the time to learn what you can about the type of business you want to start. If you are simply hoping to trade locations for the business you have already been operating, then you already have a good base of knowledge about your industry (although if you are a licensed professional and changing states or countries, you'll need to comply with the licensing requirements in the new locale). But if you are making a career change, starting a new type of business, or starting a business for the first time, you'll want to do some additional homework. While it is challenging and exciting to embark on a completely new venture, the reality is that unless you know something about your business, you're starting out a step behind your competitors.

Consider working in a similar business as the one you hope to create, even on a part-time basis. (For information about taking vacation time to try out a new business, see "Try It On for Size," below.) You will gain invaluable insight on what would be required in running a successful business, and prepare you for the entrepreneurial tasks ahead. Similarly, check out all of the educational resources that are available to you. If you're planning to open a bed and breakfast, for instance, take a class on innkeeping; if you're dreaming about opening a winery, first learn something about winemaking. The same goes for running an art gallery, opening a restaurant, or managing a catering business.

Try It On for Size

Whatever your idea or proposition, trying it out for a day, or a week, or a month can help you figure out if you and a new business are a good fit. Visit http://vocationvacations.com for hundreds of listings of jobs you can try on for a day or two for a nominal fee. If you find out that being a chocolatier isn't for you, you can also consider being an Alpaca farmer.

You may also want to look into taking classes on small business management or check out the multiple free small business resources available to you (see "Small Business Is Good for America," below). If you currently live in a more populated area, inexpensive and convenient community or adult education classes are likely available. If not, search online for Internet courses, read some books about the type of business you hope to open, or subscribe to an industry publication. Nolo also has an array of books on the practical and legal aspects of starting and managing many types of small businesses (www.nolo.com).

Small Business Is Good for America

The U.S. government supports small business by providing many free resources of business information. Start by visiting the Small Business Administration's website at www.sba.gov, which offers start-up and management advice, outlines governmental finance programs, and even offers free online courses on business topics, such as writing a business plan (see more about business plans below). The website also directs you to affiliated business information resources, such as the approximately 1,000 Small Business Development Centers located around the country, and SCORE (the Service Corps of Retired Executives, located at www.score.org), an organization of retired business executives who provide free consulting advice to any business owner.

It's no coincidence that many of the small business owners profiled in this book have previously run their own businesses. The most successful small businesses in paradise are started by owners who were able to make use of the business skills they developed beforehand—even if those skills were developed in a different industry. Consider Fiona and David Love, profiled in Chapter 4. When Fiona and David bought Candy & Kites in 2003, it had already been in business for 20 years. While Fiona and David were newcomers to the kite and candy business, they nonetheless brought with them an array of useful, related skills. They each had worked in the hotel and restaurant industry for years, and not only knew how to manage a business, but were also familiar with the tourist industry and the intricacies of running a seasonal enterprise. If that weren't enough, they spent six months working in the store and training with the owners before taking ownership of the business.

Because of this effort, Fiona reports being pleased with the decision to buy the business: "We love this new chapter in our lives," Fiona says. "Though the store keeps us busy, we do find time to hop on our tandem bike and take a ride down the coast or take our kayak out in the bay to discover the sea life."

As the Loves' experience illustrates, the more your set of skills matches the business and the more you are willing to learn about it, the more likely the business will succeed. While entrepreneurial experience is an indicator of future success in running a business, however, do not be daunted by your lack of it. That skill can be gained by working in a similar business before you start your own, being trained by the current owners of a business you hope to buy, or even on your own, if you are willing to learn. Every entrepreneur has a "first time," so you will not know until you try. Most importantly, passion goes a long way toward success. If you are truly passionate about what you are doing, that devotion will permeate all aspects of your business, and increase its chances of success. Additionally, it will make it that much easier to wake up every day and hang the "open" sign on the door.

Check With Those Closest to You

"Paradise" isn't for everybody. Your version of paradise may be physically beautiful, but depending on the location, it may sometimes feel isolated, lonely, and depending on your interests, even boring. Your dream location also offers its own challenges—while you may not miss the two-hour commutes and the rush hour traffic of the city, you may find it less than pleasant to shovel six feet of snow from your driveway in Aspen, or upon turning on the light at night in your Key West bungalow, to see a hundred or so fist-sized cockroaches scurrying across the kitchen floor. If these scenarios are unpleasant for you, just imagine how it might be for your partner or family members, whose arms you may have had to twist to consent to what they considered your hare-brained plan for paradise.

You often find family-run businesses in small resort communities, perhaps more than in larger metropolitan areas. That is fairly easy to understand—for one, the job market is narrower, so your partner, depending on his or her work experience, may not have a lot of other options. Similarly, while employees, consultants, and potential business partners are easily available in more developed areas, the human resources available in a smaller community may also be limited. While you might easily find business colleagues in a city, you're more likely to turn to your life partner as your business partner in a less-populated region.

The business/life partner combination only works, however, if your partner also enjoys the business, and if you carefully define your respective roles consistent with your respective strengths and weaknesses. Consider Vince Toreno and Patricia Martin, bed and breakfast owners profiled in Chapter 2. They both loved the idea of opening a B&B, but the business put a strain on their marriage until they defined their roles and started respecting each other's turf. Winery owners David and Patricia Coffaro provide another example. For years, Patricia was a reluctant partner in her husband's decision to open a vineyard, and she did not participate in the operation of that business. It wasn't until they converted the vineyard into a winery that she saw a role for herself in the business and plunged into the work. Her active participation has been an important component of the Coffaros' success.

> ### All in the Family
>
> Whether you're taking over a family business that's already been
> running, or starting a new one, you'll want to check out Quentin J.
> Fleming's *Keep the Family Baggage Out of the Family Business: Avoiding
> the Seven Deadly Sins That Destroy Family Businesses* (Fireside). This
> guide will show you how to separate business and family issues,
> making sure that one won't decimate the other.

The earlier that partners and family members are brought into your
plans for a business in paradise, the more likely they will support the
plan, bring their own ideas into the mix, and contribute to the success
of the business. But even if your family is not involved in the business,
make sure that they are on board with the move to paradise. This
usually means talking about the plan early and often, or as with the
Taltys (winery owners profiled in Chapter 3), introducing the family
slowly to the new community on weekends and holidays. Surprises
are usually not welcome when it means uprooting your family life.
Certainly, an unhappy family makes for a weak support structure, and
will increase your chances of failure, both in your family relationships
and in your business.

Bob Miller, the surf shop owner profiled in Chapter 4, says his wife,
Lauri, "isn't into the surf shop." But, he concedes, he couldn't have
had anywhere near the success he has enjoyed without her support and
inspiration. "She's a graduate of Berkeley, and she's just as radical as I
am. She pushes me—in every way. When we're out in the ocean, and I
see her pushing it to the limit, I think, 'I can't let her get the best wave
of the day.' She challenges me that way in my business as well."

Scout the Territory

Many people who start dreaming of a small business in paradise often do so after visiting an area as a tourist. That is a reasonable course of events, but consider that visit your "first date." When a tourist, you tend to be in a more relaxed frame of mind, and may only see the positive aspects of the community. If you're seriously considering moving to a new community and opening a business there, take a separate scouting trip during the high season—without participating in the region's tourist activities and wearing the rose-colored glasses—to see how a local resident might live. Then take a second scouting trip during the off season, so you see what life—and business—is like without the tourists.

During your scouting trips, gather information about the business community by taking note of the following:

- Is there one downtown business district where most businesses seem to be located, or are businesses spread out?
- How far is the business district from residential areas? Are customers likely to walk, drive, or take public transportation to the community's business neighborhood(s)? If they will likely arrive by car, is there ample street parking?
- Do different parts of the community appeal to different clientele?
- Are the people in the stores and on the street primarily tourists? Do they fall into a certain socioeconomic class?
- What are the peak hours for businesses in the community? Does the town shut down early at night? If so, does that bode well for the business you would like to open?
- Are there streetlights in the business district? Is crime an issue? Is there ample police and fire protection? Do the primary business districts feel safe? You may want to stop into the local police department for the local crime statistics and trends.
- Pay a visit to several businesses—what can the owners tell you about doing business there?

- How old are the buildings in town? Are businesses located within a historical district with special requirements for repair and upkeep?
- What natural forces, if any, play a factor in the area? For example, are high winds an issue? Salt air? Erosion? Ice? Forest fires? How do local businesses cope with those risks?
- Is the city well-maintained? Are the streets clean? Is the tap water drinkable?
- How do the answers to these questions differ during the community's peak season and off season?

If at all possible, try to live as a resident during these scouting trips by securing a short-term rental in an apartment or house. Run errands as you would if you lived there—go to the grocery store, post office, bank, and coffee shop. Get up and go to bed at the hours you would need to if your business was already up and running. Your personal observations on the business community and the interactions you experience with local residents will give you a sense of whether you would enjoy being a permanent member of the community. The information you gather will also help in choosing a location for your business, addressed in Chapter 7.

Gauge Market Demand and Check Out the Competition

Not every community has a need for every type of business. Say, for example, that you would like to open a sushi restaurant. However, the mere lack of a sushi restaurant in the community you have targeted doesn't indicate that there's a demand for one. Visit the local chamber of commerce to gather some statistics about the local and tourist populations—what are their respective age ranges, income levels, spending habits, and family and racial status? Do the demographics indicate a population that is likely to frequent sushi restaurants?

If there are other sushi restaurants in town, try eating as many meals as you can in those places. Observe their traffic levels. (Also note how you feel being at the same restaurant(s) a lot, because that is what you will be doing if you open a business.) If there's no exact match for the type of business you're planning to open, find something similar and gauge demand there (for instance, if there is no sushi restaurant, check out the Thai restaurant). Know that your observations may be your chief source of information—some business owners may be somewhat open to talking to you about their businesses, but less so if they identify you as a potential competitor.

Likewise, if there is competition, you'll need to look into whether or not the community can support another business of your type. Continuing with the sushi restaurant example, find out how many other sushi restaurants are in town. What is their target market? Just because they also serve sushi doesn't mean they're after the same clientele as your restaurant would be. They may cater to customers with lower—or higher—levels of disposable income, or appeal primarily to local or tourist clients. How spread out are the competitors' locations? Could a new restaurant situate itself competitively? How old is the newest sushi restaurant in town? If it's been there a while, there's likely more of an opportunity for a newcomer.

Also take a look at the broader competitive picture. Are there a lot of restaurants in town already? If so, are they always busy? Follow the same process for other lines of businesses. For instance, if you plan on opening a jet ski rental business, your competition is not only other jet ski rental shops, but other water sports businesses that compete for tourist dollars by offering alternative activities to riding jet skis.

If you feel comfortable doing so, try to speak with as many towns-people as you can to gauge their interest in the business you are considering—would they be likely to support such a business, and if so, how often? Gather up local newspapers and advertising flyers, as they often provide good information for the tastes and habits of the people in town. You may also consider subscribing to the local paper from your current residence—that way you can track from afar what local businesses are doing and which ones seem successful, and also note business opportunities arising from changes in the community. For instance, if there is a new housing development being considered in the community (and likely debated intensely in the local paper), you can start thinking about what businesses could serve that development if it is approved.

Estimate Your Start-Up Costs

With all of the useful information you have gathered, you are ready to start examining the nuts and bolts of your enterprise. One of the first tasks is to estimate your start-up costs—what's it going to take to get your business off the ground? The Internet can be a valuable resource in calculating the start-up costs for your dream business (try typing "start-up costs" along with a word or phrase describing the type of business you are interested in, such as "ski shop," "bed and breakfast," or "winery," into your search engine). Some types of costs, however, are fairly standard for starting up a business in any industry, and may include:

- **Formation costs:** If you are planning on doing business in the United States, you may, in general, structure your business as a sole proprietorship, a partnership (if there is to be more than one owner), a limited liability company (LLC), or a corporation (there are a couple of types), all of which are described more fully in Chapter 12. While the treatment and setup of these business structures vary from state to state, and other considerations play into the choice of entity, the decision will likely depend on how much protection from liability you seek, as well as how your business will be financed. Costs in setting up a corporate or LLC structure—which also provides the greatest protection from liability and most flexibility for financing—can easily run into the thousands of dollars, especially if you engage a lawyer to do the work for you. You may do it yourself—see *Legal Guide for Starting & Running a Small Business* by Fred Steingold (Nolo)—or engage an online service to help you with state registration (see www.corporate.com). Setup costs do vary greatly by state, and assuming you will be doing business in the United States, you can research them by going to the secretary of state's website for the state in which you plan to do business.

- **Licenses and permits:** At the very least, you will likely need to obtain a local business license to open your doors (city and/or county). If you are selling goods, you will likely be required to obtain a resale license (whereby you agree to collect sales taxes from customers, and pay those amounts to the state), and you may be required to post a bond to back up that promise. There may be other permits, approvals, or licenses you need to obtain in order to operate a certain type of business, sell particular products, or establish the business in a specific location. (For more about regulatory requirements, see, "Registrations, Licenses, and Permits" in Chapter 12.) Fees and other costs for complying with licensing and permit requirements vary greatly. You can start your investigation by calling the planning department of the town or county where you plan to do business, and ask for help in getting started.

- **Moving costs:** If you are relocating an existing business, get estimates from moving companies about transporting your equipment and inventory, if any. For tax record keeping, separate the costs of moving the business from the costs of moving you and your family's personal items.

- **Facilities costs:** During your scouting trips, begin looking at possible business sites and talk to commercial real estate agents to get some idea of what your facility costs will be, whether you decide to purchase or lease. See Chapter 7 for more discussion about this choice. If purchasing, your initial costs will include a down payment and closing costs. If you plan on leasing, know what is typically expected in terms of initial payments under a commercial lease in that area.

- **Remodeling:** Once you have identified a site, how much money will it take, if any, to get your building ready for your business? Are structural changes required, such as new walls or an improved ventilation system? Or are only cosmetic changes needed, such as flooring and paint? Landlords of commercial property often will agree to share or bear the cost of improvements for a business—

check to see whether that is a possibility for properties you are considering leasing.

- **Equipment and supplies:** What will you need to purchase for your business? Include everything in your estimate—from the chairs in the waiting room to the taffy machine, the wine barrels, the ceiling fan over the bar, and the new sign out front. Also include at least one month of supplies—the flour and water (or pencils and paper, or ski wax and rental slips) needed to provide your product or service.

- **Inventory:** Whether a business requires inventory, and if so, how much, varies by type of business. If you are providing a service—law, bookkeeping, therapeutic massage, or other service, inventory costs (other than goods you may sell in conjunction with your service) are not a big consideration. If you are selling any type of goods in conjunction with your service (spa products as part of your massage business), opening any type of retail store, or are manufacturing a product for resale, however, research what is considered adequate, and include the costs of starting inventory in your estimate.

- **Utilities:** Local utilities may require some form of deposit before the lights and water can be turned on, the Internet and telephone connections are made, or the garbage picked up. Inquire in advance so you're not caught off guard.

- **Insurance:** You will likely need general liability insurance, but also consider whether you should have other coverage particular to your industry or to your location, such as flood or earthquake insurance coverage. (See "Insurance" in Chapter 13 for a discussion of some of the types of policies to consider.)

- **The rainy day fund:** Once you've compiled all of your start-up costs, add on something extra to cover overhead costs while the business gets going, and for unforeseen expenses. A good rule of thumb is to calculate the cost of running your business for three months, and include that amount in your start-up costs.

Do a Break-Even Analysis

Putting start-up costs aside for a minute, now it's time to determine whether your small business in paradise can actually cover its costs (and make a profit). A simple and efficient way to determine this is by performing a break-even analysis—in other words, figuring out how much money your business will need to bring in every month to cover expenses. To do that analysis, you'll need to estimate the following amounts:

- **Fixed costs:** Also known as "overhead," these are usually monthly expenses that a business incurs simply to open its doors, and include predictable expenses such as rent, utilities, and insurance.

- **Direct costs:** These are the actual costs to you of a product or service your business will sell—for example, the wholesale cost of fishing reels at your fly-fishing shop; or the cost of the flour, butter, and eggs that will go into the cakes at your bakery.

- **Sales revenue:** This is a difficult calculation, especially if you have no experience in the particular business, and can be complicated by the human tendency to overestimate. Nevertheless, try to come up with some reasonable assumptions about what sales or income will be for a year, and then divide by 12 to get a monthly estimate. If you are not familiar with the business, research in trade websites or publications what revenues might be typical in the industry in a business similar to your own in terms of size and location. Try to be as realistic and conservative as possible.

- **Gross profit:** To calculate, subtract direct costs from sales revenue. For instance, if you paid $30 for a fishing rod, and sold it for $40, your gross profit is $10.

- **Gross profit margin:** To determine, divide the gross profit by the selling price of a given item. Using the above example, your gross profit margin would be 25% ($10 divided by $40).

- **Break-even point:** Once you've estimated all of the above numbers, you can estimate your break-even point by dividing your fixed costs by your gross profit margin. For example, if your business's fixed costs are $5,000 per month, and its gross profit margin is 25%, its break-even point—or how much you'll need to bring in each month to cover your costs—is about $20,000.

Recovering Start-Up Costs

Once you have estimated your break-even point, you can also estimate how much you'll need to earn each month in order to recoup your business start-up costs within a certain period of time. For example, if your start-up costs are $200,000, the break-even point is estimated at $20,000 per month, and you hope to recoup your start-up costs in 40 months, you would need to earn a monthly net profit (after both fixed and direct costs) of $5,000 (on total sales of $25,000 per month).

So far, you've done a lot of work—you've considered whether a business in paradise is a good fit for you and those close to you, learned more about the type of business you may want to start, checked out the community and its need for your business, and done some initial analysis about what it would cost to start your business and break even. If your dream business looks like it could work, and you still want to make a go of it, then you're ready to take the next step of creating a business plan.

Write a Business Plan—Really

Don't shut the book! Practically every experienced or novice entrepreneur dreads creating a business plan, which is a written document describing and analyzing a business and offering detailed projections about its future. While a business can get off the ground without one, most small business owners who have written business plans find them to be extremely useful. In addition to the very concrete benefit of helping you raise money (most lenders and investors will require one), a business plan helps you work through your own ideas and decide whether or not to proceed with your business at all. Think of it as running a virtual company—creating a detailed description of how your company will operate and make a profit will help you spot and solve problems on paper (which is much cheaper than in real life), can help improve upon your business concept, and keep you on track, all of which increases your chance of success. (In paradise, of course, many a rudimentary business plan is concocted at night, over cocktails, at the beach, or on the ski slopes, and often is first penned on the not-so-mythical cocktail napkin.)

The components of a formal business plan appropriate to share with potential lenders or investors in your business are listed in "Pieces of a Business Plan," below. However, know that the heart of any business plan is identifying the "problem" that your business will solve; i.e., the need that is not being adequately addressed in the community where you will do business, how your business will address that need profitably, the risks involved, and how your business will minimize those risks. Putting together a plan may sound like a lot of work, but even the owner of a thatch-roofed bar on the beach will find it useful to have a general idea where his or her business is going before setting that first stake in the sand.

A word of caution: As part of your business plan, whether you are creating a formal plan for potential lenders or simply a road map for your own use, you'll be making financial projections, forecasting what you believe your business will earn in revenue and profits. Whether or not your estimates are reasonable will depend in part on how accurate your growth forecasts are. Try to avoid one of the biggest mistakes of new small business owners—overestimating their own abilities to grow a business. Compare your growth assumptions to those of the industry you are considering, as well as the economic growth of the local paradise economy. (The local or state chamber of commerce may be able to provide you with historical growth statistics for the local economy, possibly also broken down industry by industry—and if you're lucky, by both revenue and profit.)

Pieces of a Business Plan

There are many resources—classes, books, and software—for drafting a business plan, all of which may make slightly different recommendations about what a plan requires. According to Mike McKeever, author of *How to Write a Business Plan* (Nolo), a complete business plan should start with a title page, plan summary, and table of contents, and include the following elements:

- Statement of the problem that your business is trying to solve
- Description of the business you are hoping to start
- Description of the business accomplishments of you and any other principals
- Marketing plan for your business (see Chapter 10 for creating a marketing plan)
- Sales revenue forecast for at least two years (see "Do a Break-Even Analysis," above, for a discussion of sales forecasts)
- Profit and loss forecast for at least two years (which entails a more detailed forecast to determine whether you will be profitable)
- Capital spending plan (see "Estimate Your Start-Up Costs," above, for the amount you'll need to get started in the business)
- Cash flow forecast for at least two years (see Chapter 8 to consider how the seasonality of paradise businesses affects the cash inflows and outflows of your business)
- Statement of future trends affecting the business
- Statement of risks facing the business
- Personnel plan (see Chapter 9 to consider staffing concerns for paradise businesses)
- Statement of specific business goals
- Personal financial statement
- Statement about the personal background of the founders
- Appendix with any supporting documentation.

Consider Your Financing

Unless you already have a horde of cash or other saleable assets, one of the most important aspects of planning your business is figuring out how to finance it. There are generally two types of outside financing you can seek: loans, which your business must pay back, and equity, in which investors take the risk of losing their investment in exchange for a piece of the upside potential of your business.

Many entrepreneurs shy away from equity financing for fear of giving up control over their businesses. However, taking on equity investors in your business can have many benefits. To start, an equity investor will share not only in the profits of the business, but also in the risk that the business will suffer losses or fail. An infusion of cash (or even needed equipment or other assets) from investors may speed your business's growth in a way that would not otherwise be possible. Additionally, while you will likely need to provide investors with information about the company's performance and meet with them periodically, you do not necessarily give up control of your business by taking an equity partner. Minority investments can be structured so that you, the majority owner, still make the management decisions. However, as someone in control of a business in which others have invested, you would have a fiduciary duty to those investors, and they could sue you if they suspect that you have acted dishonestly or in conflict with the interests of the business (and its other owners).

Equity investments in paradise locations may offer a particular appeal to some investors—the same lifestyle cachet that attracts a business owner can also draw investors who live elsewhere but enjoy making that twice-a-year jaunt to the winery they own a share in, or the sports store where they rent their skis. Business owners may appreciate these absentee investors precisely because they are not around all the time, not because the owners are dishonest, but because they might not like having every decision evaluated by someone who is physically present. As the owners of the Dutcher Crossing winery described in Chapter 3, equity investors may also be strong advocates for your business and a source of client referrals.

Business loans are the other primary way to finance a new business. Most lenders will require some form of collateral for the loan, usually in the form of a mortgage on your commercial property, your house, or the receivables and equipment of the business. But not always—for example, your business may qualify for Small Business Association backing, which can speed approval and help you borrow both from banks and other commercial lenders, sometimes at lower interest rates (see www.sba.gov for more information about SBA loans and guarantees). Almost any lender, however, will require a personal guarantee of repayment from the owner. Essentially this removes the protection for your personal assets that the corporate and LLC structure offers—at least with respect to the amounts owed to the lender—so borrow carefully.

Fred Steingold, in his book *Legal Guide for Starting & Running a Small Business* (Nolo), describes in detail various sources of financing, a list of which is included in "Finding Your Funding," below. The list includes drawing from personal resources (your own savings and home equity), drawing on various forms of loans and credit (anywhere from credit cards to vendor financing to commercial and bank lenders), and finding possible investors (who may include family and friends, the seller of a business you are purchasing, and venture capitalists). While retirement funds are listed as a possible source, think long and hard about using them—most financial planners would not recommend depleting those funds (see "Managing Debt" in Chapter 13 for a discussion why). Additionally, if you are considering asking friends or family members to invest in your business, you might read *Investors in Your Backyard,* by Asheesh Advani (Nolo), a guide on how to structure financing for your business with friends and family members.

Finding Your Funding

While banks are the first place you may think of turning to when you need extra funds, you may find the business funding you need by continuing to work or drawing on other resources. Some possible funding sources are:

- salary
- personal savings
- equity in your home
- retirement savings, such as a loan from your 401(k) plan
- credit cards
- buying on credit (i.e., from suppliers)
- leasing (i.e., equipment)
- friends, family, and other supporters
- banks
- other commercial lenders
- venture capitalists
- the seller of an existing business.

Have a "Plan B"

One clear pattern that emerged when interviewing business owners for this book is that many had some sort of backup plan if their experience in paradise did not turn out as they hoped. Typically, these "Plan Bs" were a second business or service that supported business owners in two ways: first, by providing income while their new businesses were getting off the ground, and second, by serving as a fallback career if the businesses in paradise failed or weren't as successful as expected. Plan B may be a business you are already involved in, as was the case with

Michael Talty, who ran his court reporting business while getting his vineyard to a profitable point. Plan B may also be something you have not done before, but is a good fit with the paradise environment, as was the case with Gordon Finwall.

Gordon is the owner of Posada del Quijote in San Jose, Costa Rica. An attorney and successful investor in Silicon Valley, he left California for Costa Rica in the early 1990s with the dream of opening a chic but cozy resort, named after the fictional Spanish character, Don Quijote. The resort is now thriving, and Gordon has handed off the day-to-day operations to a resident manager. Reaching that point took a lot longer than Gordon had expected, but his Plan B helped him hold out until he made it. While he was building his resort business, Gordon also set up a small offshore tax accounting business, which not only helped support the inn through rough times, but went on to far surpass the inn in terms of profit and revenue. Now he is preparing to sell Posada del Quijote and move to Argentina to open a winery, where once again his Plan B will support his small business in paradise.

Get Your Current House in Order

While you are planning your entry into your new life in paradise, you'll also need to plan your departure from your old one. Make sure your financial and business matters are resolved before completely pulling up roots. Wouldn't it be a shame to be sitting on the dock in front of your new fleet of deep-sea fishing vessels, and your business partner from the accounting firm you left behind in Cleveland (but still own a stake in) is being sued—and your insurance policy lapsed a month ago! In their eagerness to get to their dream lives, many people have had to leave paradise to go back and fix problems in their previous ones.

If you are leaving a business behind to start another in paradise, do not make the mistake of letting someone else wind up or sell its operations. No one knows the details of your business the way you do, so sell it or close it with the same diligence you exercised when you were running it. Similarly, if your business at home will continue and you plan to retain an equity stake, make sure you're handing off the management to people you trust, and that both you and the new management understand what your departure from day-to-day involvement means. Your agreement with them should accurately reflect your mutual understanding about your continuing responsibilities and liability for the business, if any.

If you're leaving a job as an employee, make sure you've secured your retirement plan, and rolled it over if needed. Look into extending your corporate health plan under COBRA, legislation which gives employees who lose their health coverage when leaving their jobs the opportunity to continue their group health benefits for a limited time (ask your current health group health plan administrator about COBRA or see www.dol.gov/dol/topic/health-plans/cobra.htm for more information). Perhaps most importantly, don't burn any bridges—you never know if your old job—or one like it—will turn out to be the work you prefer.

Similarly, if you're selling your house, close escrow before leaving town—problems and last-minute issues frequently arise before the closing and it is helpful if you are available to deal with them. And take heed from the old saying, "It's better to run to something, than away from something." Being finished with the old life frees you for the possibilities your new life can offer, and the success or failure of your business in paradise could depend on your freedom and availability to act on opportunities when they arise.

As this chapter has demonstrated, getting started as a small business owner in paradise can be a lot of work. However, by following these steps you have learned more about yourself, your business, and your new community, which increases your chance of success. With that under your belt, it's time to move to the next chapter—how to pick your location! ●

Finding the Right Spot in Paradise

Choosing the best location for any small business involves many considerations, including whether the property meets your business's needs, is within a reasonable distance from your home, easily accessible by customers (although accessibility may not be important depending on your type of business), and is available—whether through a lease or purchase agreement—under terms that meet your budget. Finding the right spot in paradise is no different, but there are other factors as well. For instance, while environmental risks should be considered with any property, property in paradise is more likely to be situated in a risky natural setting. The same characteristics that make a location a natural paradise (think mountains, rivers, and forests) might also create a greater risk for natural disaster (think avalanches, floods, mudslides, and forest fires). If the business will be located in a more rural setting, you may also need to learn about "country life" and how to evaluate properties outside of a metropolitan area. Additionally, if you are considering a business and property with tourists in mind, also think about whether the same property will be appealing, easily accessible, and visible to local residents during the off-peak seasons.

Perhaps the most important—and first—step in choosing property for your business in paradise, however, is to decide: "Which paradise?" Choosing what region in the world in which to do business is as much a lifestyle choice as it is a business choice.

Pick Your Paradise

To many owners of small businesses in paradise, picking a location was a "no brainer." They simply fell in love with a place they visited, and decided they would do whatever it took to build a life there. Horst Drechsler is one of those people. Growing up in Germany, Horst studied civil engineering in college. When he graduated, he could see his future laid out in front of him—he would train for a few months in a particular business, then move into an engineering post where he would spend the next 30 or 40 years.

"I realized I didn't want that kind of life," Horst says. "In Germany, everything was already planned for you. Everything was regulated. I wanted to do something that wasn't planned, something that was challenging and open-ended."

So Horst packed his bags, pocketed his life savings, and traveled the world. He toured Asia first, then Africa, and finally South America. His travels came to a halt when he landed in Brazil, where he instantly fell in love with the people and the culture of the country. Horst gradually made his way north along the coast from Rio de Janeiro until he happened upon a small island called Morro de Sao Paulo, close to the coastal city of Salvador, Bahia. That was in 1982, and back then the only way to get to the island—other than to charter a boat—was to catch a ride with the small fishing vessels that sometimes ventured there from the mainland or the occasional cargo boat that brought supplies to the people on the island.

Today, Morro de Sao Paulo remains an idyllic island with no motorized vehicles, no paved roads, no chain stores, and no Starbucks—although there is now a high-speed catamaran that takes you there in 30 minutes from Salvador. But perhaps the island's biggest allure is the people—a small collection of native Brazilians and drifters who, over the years, have come to the island on vacation and stayed. There was an influx of hippies in the sixties and seventies, then a wave of people like Horst who weren't cut out for the corporate lifestyle of the eighties. Now the island attracts Gen-Xers who would rather surf the waves than the Internet. They all share a love for the simple, eclectic, and peaceful lifestyle of Morro de Sao Paulo.

It's not difficult to imagine why Horst fell in love with the island. It is, however, difficult to imagine how he could build a thriving business in a place offering so little in the way of infrastructure or an established business community, amongst a population whose language he didn't speak. But build a thriving business is exactly what he did. Horst's Pousada Natureza is one of a handful of simple but upscale inns on Morro de Sao Paulo, which itself has transformed over the years to a more bustling resort town—though it still hasn't lost its peaceful, Xanadu-like atmosphere.

your business (not to mention your peace of mind). The decision to purchase may also help you obtain a business loan, as lenders prefer to make loans that are secured by real estate. Finally, if your business fails or you decide that it was not what you wanted to do, you can lease or sell the property.

The disadvantages of ownership include the possibility of being stuck owning property in what is considered a resort location, where property values may be more volatile and dependent on the overall health of the national economy. If the property is located where natural disasters are likely to occur, you may not want to take the risk of ownership until you have a sense of how area properties are affected by high water or strong winds. Additionally, you may be hesitant to invest in property for a business and/or in a community new to you—if you find that you don't enjoy the antiques business after all, and the community feels more like Hooterville (and not in a good way) than the bucolic retreat you had hoped for, owning property may feel like an unwanted barrier to departure.

Consider Seller Financing

If you would like to own your business property but are concerned with financing, know that some sellers may consider financing all or part of the purchase, whereby you would pay off the loan to the seller, with interest as you would with another lender. (An especially adventurous lender may even be interested in taking a piece of your business for a reduction in the selling price.) It all depends on the seller—if he or she owns the property outright (has no mortgage) and does not need the cash immediately from the sale of the property, seller financing is a possibility. A seller may actually prefer this private lending arrangement if he or she earns interest at a rate higher than other available interest-bearing investments and the loan is secured by an interest in the business property. At any rate, it never hurts to ask!

Creating a Priorities Checklist

For whatever reason—either because financing is not a possibility or other concerns, many new business owners in paradise choose to lease rather than buy. Whether buying or leasing, however, your next step is to decide what features you are looking for in a business property. (If you have already scouted out the community, you probably already have some ideas about what you want.)

If you are planning on leasing, Janet Portman and Fred Steingold, authors of *Negotiate the Best Lease for Your Business* (Nolo), suggest creating a rental priorities worksheet before looking for rental property. Conversely, if you have decided to purchase property, you'll benefit from creating a similar document for your purchase requirements. While creating a priorities list may seem like unnecessary work, it forces you to articulate what you want before meeting with brokers or other individuals who might be motivated to get a property leased or sold without considering all of your requirements. Additionally, you will be less likely to commit to a property that, while appealing, clearly doesn't meet your business's needs.

To create your priorities worksheet, write down all of the essential features your property must have, followed by your compromise items—features you would like but aren't crucial, and then your "unacceptables"—features you absolutely want to avoid. Likely the "must-have" section of your worksheet will start with financial terms—the maximum rent or purchase price your business can afford. Additionally, most businesses need basic electrical, plumbing, and heating infrastructure, building security, and maintenance. After these basic requirements, different types of businesses have their own specific needs. A gallery may require a location near other galleries, a restaurant owner may be concerned about picking a spot with a view and a personality, a CPA or an orthodontist might want a centrally located office downtown, and a wine wholesaler might require loading docks and easy access by delivery trucks. Your business property checklist will likely include other must-have features, some of which may be related to the property characteristics listed below:

- Commuting time to your home
- Access to public transportation
- Neighbors and the neighborhood
- Size of the property and physical attributes
- Noise levels and traffic
- Restroom facilities
- Storage space
- Parking
- Image and maintenance
- Expansion or purchase potential
- Zoning compliance.

Continue your list with the items you'd like to have but that aren't crucial (such as specific features of the property's appearance), and follow with the list of unacceptable features of the property (for instance, you may know that you do not want your business in a mall or where there is no public transportation).

Starting the Search

Once you have your preliminary list of priority items, start looking for a broker in the area. Ask people you know for recommendations. Let them know you're looking for someone honest, accessible, and with plenty of experience in the area. If they've worked with the broker before, ask them what their strong and weak points were. Would they use the same broker again? Once you identify a few brokers, ask them about their experience with commercial property. Also ask about their compensation practices, and about any conflicts of interest they might have that could favor the property owner or seller over you. Also, if the contract you sign is with a firm rather than a specific agent or broker, make sure the contract identifies the person who will represent you.

Keep in mind also that no broker is going to think through your purchase or lease for you. The most effective way to work with a real estate professional is by knowing what you want (by creating your priorities checklist, of course) and becoming familiar with regional property issues. For instance, as you learn about the area, you'll learn what questions to ask and what property features to investigate. If you are leaving a city to live in a rural setting for the first time, you may need to learn more than you care to about septic tanks, propane tanks, and well water. Properties located in the country vary greatly in the availability and quality of utilities and other services, so do not assume anything and do not be afraid to ask what sound like obvious questions. Otherwise, the lessons can be harder, as you discover that your septic tank backs up when the rainy season starts, the well that supplies irrigation water to your vineyard goes dry every August, or that garbage pickup is not available and your business duties include hauling your trash to the dump every week.

Keeping Mother Nature in mind, also make sure to perform a thorough investigation of the nature of the property during all seasons. Is it located in a flood zone? Is it susceptible to forest fires, mudslides, frequent electrical outages, mold, wind or saltwater damage? Will it likely be snowed in? If so, whose responsibility is it to plow the parking lot or the walkway? Is that idyllic property you saw in the fall—so beautiful and peaceful in its little valley—in the middle of a window-rattling, icy wind tunnel in the winter?

Negotiating a Lease

If you plan on leasing instead of purchasing and have found the right property for your business, your next step will be to negotiate the lease. The best preparation for negotiating a particular lease is gathering as much information as possible about the factors affecting the lease terms—how active the market is, what lease terms are typical for the area, the reputation of the landlord, and the history of the property.

Some of the market information will already be known to you from looking at properties, but once you've settled on a particular property, talk to the neighbors, former tenants, or current tenants if there are other units in the building. Speak to other realtors. Your investigation will reveal how much negotiating power you have and how quickly you'll need to act. If the property is indeed in high demand, you'll want to know that so you avoid raising too many issues with the landlord. If a landlord sees you as "too much trouble" in a field with many other potential tenants, they are likely to lease the property to someone else. Learning what typical lease terms are from property brokers will make you better prepared to act on a good deal when it presents itself.

Similarly, knowing the landlord's reputation will help you know what—or if—to negotiate. If the landlord has a history of problems with tenants, you may want to think twice about leasing there. "You'll often have to work very closely with your landlord. If you get the feeling that it's not going to work, walk away," attorney Janet Portman advises. Finally, investigating the property's history will help you understand its challenges and whether it will serve your needs. For instance, if you are planning on starting a restaurant and a previous restaurant has failed in that location, you will at least want to know why that has occurred. If local residents tell you it was just bad food, then you can plan on doing better. But if you learn that there was a rat infestation or the ventilation was inadequate and the place smelled like mildew, you can negotiate with the landlord to address those problems (assuming you still want to lease the property).

What to Expect

When your background work is done and you are ready to start negotiating, keep in mind that there is no such thing as a standard lease. Commercial leases vary greatly in length and terms, and are quite different from residential leases. The good news is that almost every item in a lease is negotiable. The caution is that, if you are not familiar with commercial leases and their terms, you may not know what to expect. In fact, you may find yourself in two very different negotiating scenarios:

The handshake lease. If your idea of paradise is a small town in the mountains of Tennessee or a remote beach community on the Oregon coast, you may find that business is done very casually. The owner may not have a written lease agreement and may consider a handshake or an oral agreement sufficient to seal the deal. Handshake deals work wonderfully as long as each side agrees as to what the agreement actually was. Disagreements that can't be ironed out often end up in court. Oral agreements may be valid and enforceable by a court but they are not a good choice, because both landlord and tenant have no way of knowing how a judge will rule. While not always the case, if you are new to a community and your landlord is powerful or has been living there for his or her entire life, your voice or opinion may be "a little less equal" than the landlord's in a property dispute. The solution to avoiding these problems is to insist on a lease.

"Without a lease, or with a short one-page lease, you could get into more trouble because of what isn't said than what is," says Portman. In such situations, "diplomatically introduce the topic of a lease. Or show up with your own lease. Suggest that both parties run it by their lawyers." To broach this difficult subject, you do not need to be disingenuous, but you could plead ignorance about local customs (you are ignorant, after all) and say you want to be certain you understand how the relationship works; or you could say your lawyer friend/spouse/ cousin (you can always blame the lawyers!) will berate you if you don't put the lease terms in an agreement; or you could simply say that your own personal experience has been that better business relationships are formed when all of the terms are spelled out in writing.

Know that any lease agreement should at least include the following pieces of information: the names of the landlord and tenant (if you're using a preprinted form, make sure all of the blanks are filled in), a detailed description of the property and what it includes (for instance, specify any storage space or the number of parking spaces allocated to your rental), how the rent is calculated (under many commercial leases, the tenant may be responsible for part of the property taxes, utilities, and insurance, and maintenance of common areas), when the lease begins and ends, the security deposit, what happens when the lease ends, restrictions and requirements on the rented space, insurance coverage and indemnity, building security and maintenance and who pays for them, alterations and repair policies, subletting policies, what happens if one party or the other fails to live up to the terms of the lease, a summary of how any disputes will be resolved, and who pays attorney's fees related to the disputes.

The other kind of lease. On the opposite end of the spectrum is what can summarily be referred to as "the 18-page lease," written for the occasion by an attorney or purchased as a canned form. It may only be seven or 12 pages long, but whatever its length, is filled with so many bells and whistles that it would challenge a lawyer, let alone a small business owner. You may encounter this type of document in a small rural town or in a sophisticated and bustling resort town such as Lake Tahoe or Aspen—these forms are readily available in stationery stores and from any lawyer with a form book in his library. If a laid-back landlord in a small town presents you with such a lease, you may be able to negotiate away some of the more onerous clauses. However, in big, well-established resort areas, you are more likely to be dealing with national real estate franchises and real estate attorneys instead of small-town landlords and independent realtors. These professional negotiators are proficient at convincing potential tenants that a particular property is in high demand and they would be lucky to get it, under whatever terms are offered. If the particular rental market is "hot"—properties are in short supply and rented quickly when available—you may find yourself feeling pressured to sign a complicated lease with little or no negotiation.

In such situations, make sure you seek professional help. "If you don't, you could find yourself in a very disadvantageous situation," Portman says. Portman emphasized that even if properties are going fast and you do not seem to have a strong negotiating position, talking to an attorney about the lease will at least inform you what will happen under various scenarios, such as if you want to extend the lease or improve the property. "The best leases are those without surprises," she adds.

Whatever the length of the lease agreement—whether a preprinted agreement from a stationery store, an 18-page commercial agreement from a lease broker, or something in between—remember the lease is a legal document. Don't take it lightly, no matter how casual the circumstances, as every lease creates legal obligations for you. Commercial leases typically are for five- or ten-year periods, so it will govern your tenancy for quite some time.

FIND OUT MORE

Whether reviewing a confusing or complicated lease or one that seems to have a lot missing, check out *Negotiate the Best Lease for Your Business*, by Janet Portman and Fred Steingold, for help in negotiating the lease you want.

Getting the Lease You Need

Depending on the activity in the market or the power of the landlord, you may not have much choice about lease terms. However, nothing in a lease is set in stone, so be creative about terms that fit your needs (or your concerns). For instance, if you are unsure about your commitment to the business or the community, ask for a shorter initial term (for instance, one to three years), with a longer renewal term. You never know when a term will be agreeable to the property owner (they may have other plans for the property that do not go into effect for a couple of years, and would welcome a shorter lease).

Similarly, if you will be doing business in a seasonal resort town where income or sales will fluctuate wildly from season to season, you may also want to ask for a lease with higher lease payments during peak season, and lower ones during the off season. Some resort towns—and landlords—are accustomed to such agreements.

A riskier alternative is to ask for rent payments that are tied to the success of your business. You pay a minimum amount based on the square footage, and an additional amount, called "percentage rent," that kicks in if your business hits a certain level of profitability or sales. This approach can be complicated, in that you are essentially asking the landlord to become your business partner. As such, he or she will want access to your financial records, and depending on the landlord, may want some input into, or control over, how you are operating the business.

Subleasing is an alternative way to test out your business without making a long-term commitment. Subleasing is most appropriate with businesses that are compatible in the same space (such as those relying primarily on office space), whereby the property can be fairly easily divided (either in space by using office cubes or temporary room dividers, or in time, where one or more psychotherapists or aestheticians, for example, may alternate use). An advantage to a sublease is that it is often possible to negotiate a shorter-term commitment—year to year or even month to month—giving you more flexibility in the event that your business doesn't do well. Also, with a sublease, a property's infrastructure is likely already in place, allowing your business to piggyback on some of the services that the primary tenant is using, such as an Internet hookup, janitorial services, and electricity. The primary disadvantage of a sublease is that you are at the mercy of the main tenant (and the terms of its lease with the landlord). If the primary tenant's business is growing, and your firm is growing, you are likely to be pushed out of your space at an inconvenient time.

These are examples of ways to negotiate a lease that works for you and your business. However, wherever you choose to settle, whatever location you select, and whether you lease or buy, remember that the underlying reason for living and working in paradise is to enhance your life rather than compromise it. As such, take the advice of other residents of paradise, and do not settle on a mediocre lease, a mediocre site, or a mediocre version of paradise. "Location. Location. Location. It sounds cliché, but it's so important," says winery owner Michael Talty. ●

A Business for All (or Most) Seasons

Most businesses experience some seasonality—for instance, the holiday season is by far the busiest time of year for almost all retail businesses. Businesses in paradise may also experience a holiday rush, but because of their nature and/or location, may experience other fluctuations related to weather and the tide of tourists flowing in and out of the community. Even if your business doesn't have widely different peak and low seasons—understanding local seasonal trends can help you manage your business more effectively, and make a difference to your bottom line. (For instance, if you are a CPA in a tourist community, you may not be on the "front line" of tourism, but understanding seasonal effects on your customers—local businesses—will help you be more effective in your work with them.)

As other owners of businesses in paradise have proven, managing a seasonal business can be profitable, but requires an understanding of those seasons and a plan for managing the wide variations in cash flowing in and out of your business. A plan that works will include "making hay while the sun shines"—maximizing the income of your high season(s)—and minimizing your expenses during the off season(s).

While seasonal businesses present more of a roller coaster ride in terms of cash flow management, they offer an important benefit to their owners—some down time—that year-round businesses do not. If you are hoping to start your small business in paradise in order to create a more reasonable—and varied—lifestyle, a seasonal business may be the right fit for you. This chapter will review the ways that owners of small businesses in paradise can address the risks and enjoy the benefits of the seasonality of their businesses.

Knowing Your Seasons

You already learned the seasons in kindergarten, right? Yes, but perhaps not in regard to your future business. Owners of successful seasonal businesses have a clear understanding of the length and nature of their seasons and a plan for managing the income highs and lows. Knowing the months when you are likely to make most of your income, and estimating how much you are likely to earn, is the heart of this plan, and requires taking into account both the overall seasonal trends in the community you've chosen, as well as the seasonality of your chosen line of business.

Resort community seasons usually depend on . . . the seasons, of course. You may have a general idea of the local weather patterns based on your scouting trips and casual discussions with local residents. As part of developing your seasonal plan, however, you may want to do some additional research on how many peak months your business is likely to experience. For example, if you're in a snow belt, you may want to gather historical weather patterns for when, on average, the first snow falls and the last, as well as average annual snowfall, and the number of days that roads to your community were impassable. Likewise, businesses in sunbelts will want to know how long the warm weather tends to last, and those in tropical areas will want to chart typical rainfall and storm patterns. (Looking at historical weather patterns may also indicate a shift in those patterns, and you'll want to be aware of those long-term trends, too. Global warming, for example, may already be shortening the winter ski seasons at some resorts.)

For business purposes, however, community seasons also involve the local events calendar. Familiarity with a community's festivals and other events will help you identify opportunities for your business, even if they occur outside your business's high season, weather-wise. For instance, you may own a ski shop that does most of its business in the winter, but the particular community in which it is located puts on a summer film festival—your business might pick up some extra income providing a different service or set of products during the festival.

Your particular line of business will have its "seasons" as well, many of which have less to do with the weather and more to do with holidays and your customers' patterns. For example, January is typically a horrible month for retail businesses, as it comes right after Christmas, but it's usually a good month for financial planners, self-help programs, and personal trainers, as people get themselves ready for the New Year. February is traditionally the slowest month of the year for most businesses, but during that month, there is a three-day weekend, Presidents' Day, which is generally good for resort areas, and Valentine's Day, which usually represents a bump in income for any business catering to romance, whether a restaurant, bed and breakfast, or gift, lingerie, or wine shop. March is a big month for college students taking their spring breaks, but conversely, is also a time when, according to a study in *American Demographics* magazine, attendance at church and other religious activities jumps 60%. Consequently, if you own a retreat center, March might be a high season for your business. October—Halloween month—is likely a busy season for at least the candy side of Candy & Kites, the Bodega Bay store profiled in Chapter 4. You get the idea—think about each month of the year and whether it offers income opportunities for your business.

Creating Your Plan

When you feel you have a good understanding about all aspects of your business's seasonality, put together a document that charts the likely seasonal ups and downs by month. (If you have already created cash flow projections as part of the business plan described in, "Write a Business Plan—Really" in Chapter 6, your work here might already be off to a good start. Alternatively, thinking more about your business's seasons might cause you to go back and revise those projections.)

While it's impossible to know exactly what you'll be taking in and spending each month, try to come up with a rough estimate as to how much you'll make during the peak months and low months. Compare that with the amounts you estimate will go out each month. Your goal here is to figure out how much cash you'll need to make when business is good in order to cover you through all the seasons. This analysis will serve you in several ways. First, it will help you avoid the temptation to overspend when times are good—the low season is always around the corner, and just as a high season can be better than expected, a low season can be lower than you anticipate. Second, you'll learn roughly how much shortfall—cash-wise—you are likely to experience through the year. Establish a separate reserve account in that amount to help sustain the business during the slow months. See also "Get a Line of Credit," below. (Make sure that your personal budget takes into account the highs and lows of the business. You may want to lower your own salary during the lean months, for example.) Third, your analysis will help you start thinking about how to increase your income—whether in high season or low—as well as where you might reduce expenses.

Get a Line of Credit

Most small businesses rely on a line of credit to help them smooth seasonal peaks and valleys. Even if you think you will have a cash reserve to get you through a low season, lines of credit can provide peace of mind by your knowing you won't have to shut your business with an unusually slow season or an unexpected loss. Their true beauty is in their flexibility—you draw on the line exactly when you need the money and in the exact amount you need—and can pay it back as soon as your business picks up again. Like most forms of financing, lines of credit are most easily obtained before you need it, so you may want to set it up when starting your business. Of course, similar to other debt, you'll be on the hook for paying it back (a bank will probably require a personal guarantee from you), so don't draw down more than you can realistically pay back.

If you have not yet created a cash flow projection, think of it as you would a personal budget. You can set up a simple one on a Microsoft *Excel* spreadsheet (or in Intuit *QuickBooks*,® if you have it). On the top horizontal line of the spreadsheet, list out the months of the year. In the far left vertical column, list the items that represent cash in and cash out each month. Start with your estimated monthly income. Then list the costs that vary by month, such as inventory and employee costs, and follow with expenses that don't vary and would be considered overhead, such as rent and insurance. For each item you've listed, estimate an amount and enter it into the box corresponding to the appropriate month. Subtracting your expenses—"cash out" items—from your "cash in" will give you an idea of how much cash you'll end up with, or need, that month.

While this is a very rudimentary cash flow analysis, it may be all you need to start analyzing where you can cut costs, or, keeping in mind the seasons and opportunities of your business, where you can focus on increasing your revenue. You may even decide that it just doesn't make economic sense to stay open every month of the year, and that's fine (although other variables—such as employee and customer relationships—may dictate otherwise). Coming up next are various ways that seasonal business owners manage their revenues and costs to make their businesses work for them.

Product and Service Planning

One important aspect of seasonal business planning is figuring out your mix of products and services for each season. While many types of businesses vary their offerings around the year, businesses in areas dependent on weather patterns may see the most extreme changes in their products and services—and even in their customers. Snow removal businesses switch to landscaping during the summer months, while ski resorts become summer camps oriented to hiking, fishing, art, or personal growth seminars. A hardware store will offer more garden equipment for the summer, and snow blowers and fireplace supplies for the winter. A nursery adds poinsettias and Christmas trees during the holidays and typically clears out some of its lawn products in the fall to make room for firewood and salt for icy driveways.

Jan Peterson of Jan's Mountain Outfitters, described in Chapters 9 and 11, brings in entirely new inventory for the summer months. Jan's bread and butter has always been selling sporting goods and apparel for winter sports, but over the years he has built a summer business around biking, camping, backpacking, fly fishing, and golf . The business has also diversified its services, leading sporting excursions such as fly-fishing and backpacking trips. The result: What was almost exclusively a winter sports business now brings in 30% of its revenue during the summer months.

Even businesses that may not seem to be seasonal can diversify their products and services to increase revenue. A burger restaurant might offer the "best" hot chocolate and warm desserts in winter, and the "best" milkshakes and lemonade in summer. A financial services firm may do a good part of its business in the months of December and January when clients are taking year-end distributions and planning their finances for the coming year, but many such firms expand into tax preparation or tax consulting through April. They may also take on corporate clients, which are more active year-round, or build a service around midyear portfolio rebalancing.

A SMALL BUSINESS IN Paradise

For more about Jan's Mountain Outfitters and its products and services, visit www.jans.com.

Seasonal Promotions

Like varying your product mix, seasonal promotions offer small businesses in paradise another way to increase revenue in the high season, and squeeze more revenue out of the low season. Preseason sales can help gauge demand for particular products and kick off your peak buying season, while end-of-season clearances can make room on your shelves for next season's inventory. Some businesses creatively offer customers weather guarantees on certain products. For example, a snowmobile or a snow blower may come with a guarantee that the business will refund the customer's money if that year's snowfall doesn't reach a certain level. Setting the guaranteed snow level well below the average snowfall minimizes the risk to the business, but may provide on-the-fence buyers the encouragement they need to make the commitment. Similarly, hunting and fishing supply stores may offer guarantees related to the fishing and hunting seasons established by government regulators, which seasons vary year to year depending on the availability of fish and game.

Wineries in the Dry Creek Valley wine region, as well as in other areas of the country, work together to create more traffic in their low season. Both Michael Talty and David Coffaro, winery owners profiled in Chapter 3, participate in coordinated events such as barrel tastings and wine and food "passport" weekends that draw crowds during the winter months, when the flood of regular tourists slows to a trickle. If your community doesn't offer such an event, you may consider staging one of your own (see Chapter 11 for more on event planning). Even better, trying to work with community members to start such an event may help promote your business and acquaint you with fellow business owners in the region.

Managing Inventory

If your business will carry inventory, you will find that good seasonal business planning requires making sure you have enough inventory to meet your demand during peak times, without having too much left on the shelves or on order during the slow season. The general goal in inventory management is keeping inventory as low as possible while still having enough to meet demand. Too much inventory ties up capital and requires storage space, which can be costly. Not carrying excess inventory also allows for more flexibility in your product lines, in the event that consumer tastes change or you decide to change direction in your product mix.

Most suppliers are accustomed to dealing with some seasonality no matter what the business is, so varying your orders throughout the year should not be a problem. Nevertheless, vendors appreciate knowing when to expect a slowdown in your orders so they are not overproducing a product. For instance, Fiona and David of Candy & Kites plan their inventory long in advance, and let suppliers know when to expect a ramp-up and slowdown in orders. Establishing and maintaining good relationships with vendors can help you in various ways, including by reducing the chance that you will be hampered by a short supply of your best products during a peak season. Additionally, vendors can be valuable sources of information and advice on managing your inventory—they are working with many sellers of their product and can let you know not only which products in their line are selling best, but also recommend how the products are displayed.

Create an Off-Season Business

If you believe the business cannot succeed without additional income in the slow season, or you have a lot of energy to burn, you may decide to create a separate business that operates during the off-season. You may pursue something completely different—for instance, leading river rafting tours or dusting off your house painting skills when closing your ski shop for the summer. However, if you can find a way to earn money that is related to your core business, it will help build your business's brand in the community while adding to business income.

For example, Ginger Carlton, the restaurateur profiled in Chapter 5, has built a successful catering business around the film industry. Filmmakers tend to choose the off season to film in Hawaii, when there aren't as many tourists to get in the way. Ginger made a concerted effort to market her catering services to filmmakers coming to Kauai, researching which films were planning to film on the island and contacting them by phone and with mailers before their arrival. Now, they call her in advance to engage her on-location catering services. Her restaurant and catering businesses work well together—the success of her restaurant adds to her credibility as a caterer when seeking new catering contracts. (Similarly, during the season when most filming takes place, her restaurant business is slow and she can rely on her staff to manage while she's working at filming locations.) Conversely, the catering business brings more customers in—film crew members who taste her cooking on the set are likely to visit Caffe Coco, and refer others. The two businesses support each other and make maximum use of Ginger's employees and skills.

Make Use of the Off Season

An advantage of having a seasonal business is that you have time between seasons to do the long-term planning and projects that many year-round businesses never have time to do. Business guru Stephen Covey (author of *The Seven Habits of Highly Effective People* (Free Press)) refers to these as "Quadrant Two" activities—important but not urgent tasks that include business planning, physical refurbishing of the business, education and training (for you and your workers), relationship building, and taking time to renew yourself. Just because customers may be scarce is no reason to write off the slow season as unproductive—you will finally have time to accomplish tasks that will serve you and your business well over the long term.

Patricia Martin and Vince Toreno, bed and breakfast owners profiled in Chapter 2, spend the off season remodeling and doing necessary repairs to the rooms in their B&B, attending seminars and community networking events, working on their website, and making plans for the next and future seasons. Using the off season to catch up with long-term projects—so difficult to do with a year-round business—allows Patricia and Vince the luxury of focusing exclusively during peak season on their customers and day-to-day management of the business.

Of course, one of the most important activities to pursue during the off season is self-renewal. Just think, scheduling your vacations during the off season may mean you will be avoiding vacation crowds! And taking a breather will refresh you for the next high season. Some seasonal businesses find it most efficient—and cost-effective—to close the business down entirely for a couple of weeks or more in the offseason, while encouraging their workforce to take their vacations at the same time. The owners get the break they need, without missing a lot of business.

In addition to the strategies described in this chapter, there are two other important components of managing your business's seasonality, both of which make a big difference to the bottom line. The first has to do with managing a seasonal work force—clearly, your business expenses can vary greatly with the number of temporary workers you hire, but at the same time, not hiring enough workers will likely cost you in terms of revenue. Striking the right balance is discussed in Chapter 9. The second component comprises your marketing and community involvement efforts. Both are integral to increasing your business's presence and ultimately, its revenues, and are addressed in Chapters 10 and 11.

Owners of seasonal businesses know that the key to making the business work is not to fight the seasons, but embrace them. Use these peaks and valleys to your advantage, planning your business so that it—and you—derive as much benefit as possible from the high seasons, and make efficient—and possibly life-enhancing—use of the slow times. ●

CHAPTER

9

Staffing Paradise

People who set up business in paradise are often surprised to find that practices in hiring, managing, and retaining employees are different than those involved in staffing a business in more metropolitan areas. For example, the best place to find candidates may not be websites such as www.monster.com or www.careerbuilder.com, but the bulletin board at the local coffee shop; the most-valued incentive pay may not be a performance-based bonus, but free lift tickets to the local ski resort; and the definition of a long-term employee may be ten months instead of ten years. Managing a workforce in paradise can take some getting used to for an employer fresh from a metropolitan area.

One of the biggest challenges is that many resort-type businesses are staffed by transient, seasonal workers who show up for the busy months to work (and play), and then leave. The benefit of this schedule for employers is that workers are available during the peak season months, when business is strong and the need for employees is higher. But the seasonal availability of workers also presents several obstacles. Finding seasonal workers can be difficult for small businesses that don't have the name recognition of a large ski resort or retail chain, for example. If a new applicant doesn't walk in the front door, how do you go about locating them? And when you do find them, training an entirely new temporary workforce every year can be a human resources nightmare—not to mention the attendant risk of major gaps in customer service resulting from rushed or insufficient training. Additionally, while some of the fun of working with temporary workers arises from their varied background—many may come from other countries—cultural differences and language barriers may result in unexpected difficulties. Finally, many temporary workers take their jobs a bit less seriously than year-round employees, and that attitude can result in conflicts between the seasonal staff and what you may consider your core employees. Managing what is essentially two workforces—one temporary and requiring intense oversight, the other more long-term and requiring more traditional human resource management skills—would challenge anyone.

What's more, workers in paradise—be they seasonal or year-round—tend to have a very different mindset than workers in less seasonal locations. As someone considering opening shop in paradise, you understand the appeal of intangible benefits such as being able to walk out the front door and gaze onto a mountain stream, a vineyard, or a white-sand beach, biking to work, cutting out early to ski, or closing shop when the marlin are biting. In short, you may be starting a small business is paradise in order to reach a better balance between your work and your life. The key to being a successful manager of people in a resort location is to realize that your employees want the same things that you do. The wait staff, the bookkeeper, and the sales clerk have all chosen to live in paradise because they, too, value a certain quality of life. Getting in the way of their enjoyment of that life is a sure-fire way to a disgruntled staff.

There's a Lot of Law Involved in Hiring Workers

Numerous federal, state, and local laws affect employers depending on the location, size, and type of business, the particular type of work, the seasonality of it, whether the work is full- or part-time, year-round or temporary, and more. These laws affect all aspects of employment, including screening and hiring, pay and benefits, and terminations and layoffs. Chapter 12 provides an overview of the payroll tax issues related to employees, but for complete details about how to hire and manage employees, see *The Employer's Legal Handbook*, by Fred Steingold (Nolo). The U.S. Department of Labor website (www.dol. gov) also offers a wealth of information about how to comply with federal employment laws (and may also refer you to the related state law as well). To avoid legal hassles, make sure you know and comply with the law—and that your employees know the score as to the terms of your employment arrangement.

The Seasonal Workforce

For many proprietors, transient workers are a necessary but frustrating element of their business. They are necessary because the local permanent population simply is not large enough to fill high-season staffing needs. Additionally, it's more than just the retail and wait staff positions that require filling during peak seasons. While many of the available seasonal jobs are within the retail, hospitality, and sporting industries, there are a myriad of other businesses that provide infrastructure and services and also have a need for additional staff during the high season. Therefore, the high season creates a ramp-up in demand for many types of workers—from clerical and financial positions to housekeeping and event planning.

Employers often find a transient workforce brings frustrations too, chiefly related to the fact that it is usually made up of young, ill-trained workers who are more interested in hitting the slopes with their friends—or skipping out to the local night life—than in earning a living or, perish the thought, building a career. Bob the Surfer from Chapter 5, for example, tends to hire other surfers to work in his shop. But when the waves are high, they all want to be someplace else, and there is no assurance they will return. (Bob recalls one of his best employees going to Costa Rica to surf one holiday, falling in love with another surfer there, and never coming back.)

Finding Employees

Bob's dilemma represents one of the greatest difficulties reported by business owners in paradise—staying adequately staffed during wildly fluctuating business seasons. While most resort locations have one high season per year to deal with temporary staffing challenges, the thriving resort community of Whistler, British Columbia, enjoys two strong tourist seasons each year—winter and summer. In winter, thousands of people come from all over the world to ski and snowboard at one of the world's top winter resorts, which includes the majestic and challenging Blackcomb Glacier. In summer, outdoor sports ranging from mountain biking and kayaking to fly fishing and moose hunting attract a second round of tourists that's almost as large as the winter crowds.

The dual season is a good thing for business owners, of course, because it ensures a steady flow of customers almost year-round. However, Whistler employers may be doubly challenged. While it seems that an almost year-round business would be more likely to have almost all year-round employees, it has not yet worked that way. Whistler doesn't have nearly enough full-time residents to handle either the winter or the summer crowds. Typically, different sets of seasonal workers are

A SMALL BUSINESS
IN *Paradise*

For more information about Whistler's Personnel Solutions, go to www.whistler-jobs.com.

available for the winter and summer seasons, so Whistler employers are challenged by hiring two sets of seasonal workers every year.

"Whether you're involved in the tourist industry directly or not, all the businesses in Whistler revolve around these seasons," says Cathy Goddard, founder and owner of Whistler's Personnel Solutions. Cathy's mission is making sure that other businesses in Whistler have the right workers—and the right number of them—throughout the year. Cathy moved to Whistler in the late 1980s, and founded the agency in 1995 after recognizing local businesses' need for year-round, well-trained employees. Cathy is very involved in her community—she's a board member of the Women of Whistler, a businesswomen's networking group, writes a weekly human resources column for the *Whistler Question* newspaper and Vancouver's *Employment Paper*, and speaks at numerous human-resources-related workshops and seminars.

"The key to staffing a business in a resort community is to have the right mix of well-trained staff and transient workers," Cathy says. Her firm hires both for local employers—Whistler Personnel Solutions recruits full-time, perennial workers, and serves as a temporary employment agency addressing short-term and seasonal staffing needs.

Start Locally When Hiring Workers—Then Expand Your Territory

An Internet search for "staffing" or "human resources" or "employment agency" along with the name of your community can turn up companies, such as Whistler's Personnel Solutions, that offer staffing services in a given area. Local chambers of commerce and business organizations such as the Rotary Club should also be able to supply you with a list of staffing resources or alert you to a job board in the area. (These organizations can also be valuable resources for planning your workforce and helping you determine appropriate compensation levels and benefits.) Your website (if any) is a good place to list employment opportunities. Jan's Mountain Outfitters (discussed below) has an online employment application that makes it easy for people to apply for a job. Classifieds in specialty magazines and newsletters (for skiers, climbers, divers, golfers, and the like) may also be terrific resources for your business. You might also advertise in selected university and college publications, particularly those whose students might be interested in working in your business (for instance, a ski resort may advertise in the student newspapers for the University of Colorado and Colorado State University, where there are likely a lot of students interested in skiing). Craigs List (http://sfbay.craigslist.org) is a great and reasonably priced way to recruit employees from throughout the U.S., and even many countries. Finally, don't forget retired workers who may be fine doing seasonal or part-time work. Check out the AARP's Employer Resource Center at www.aarp.org/money/careers/employerresourcecenter for advice on tapping into this market.

As the case with many resort locations, hundreds of transient workers flock to Whistler every year from places as far away as Argentina, Australia, and Europe. Some of them come for the summer, others for the winter. Major employers such as the Whistler-Blackcomb Ski Resort work with international employment services to hire people for seasonal jobs and internships, such as www.interexchange.org, which places primarily university students and other young workers from around the world in three-to-four-month seasonal jobs. Most of Whistler's small businesses, however, do no planning or scheduling around this migration of workers. The workers simply show up looking for jobs at the beginning of the season. They compete with each other for the available jobs, and the small businesses compete for their services. After the season is over, most of them go back home.

Start Early When Hiring Seasonal Workers

While many small businesses do not recruit seasonal workers, making an effort to hire workers before your competition might yield you the most competent and responsible temporary employees. Transient workers tend to start arriving just ahead of the tourist crowds each season. Within a few weeks, though, most of them will already have jobs, so it pays to advertise your job openings early and actively seek employee referrals at least a month before the season begins. If at all possible, line up next season's workers a full year beforehand, before the current year's seasonal employees go home.

Working With Temporary Employees

Temporary workers fill temporary needs and also offer another advantage—they tend to work for lower wages and fewer benefits than the local population. What's more, they may offer their own attraction, as many tourists have come to expect and to enjoy the foreign accents and international flavor of the transient workforce. Many employers such as ski resorts take advantage of this by printing the worker's birthplace on their nametags—and there's no reason a small business owner can't use the same practice.

The difficulty for employers in paradise is is finding workers who have relevant work experience and a sense of responsibility and commitment. (Your employees must also be able to prove they have the legal right to work in the U.S. See "Workplace Laws and Regulations" in Chapter 12 for more discussion on documents employees need to fill out for their employer.) One way to address your hiring difficulties is engaging employment agencies such as those described above to help find appropriate employees. Another way is to cultivate transient workers who are likely to return for more than one season. Repeat employees tend to be more valuable because they do not require as much training during subsequent seasons. Start seeking return employees by asking job candidates about their future plans in their initial interviews. It is not difficult to tell the difference between a young applicant who simply loves travel and adventure, and one who has a genuine interest in the locale and plans to return.

Other ways to bring good seasonal workers back include offering higher wages in subsequent seasons, or end-of-season bonuses that go up every year. Some business owners offer lodging incentives—some small business owners even bring workers into their homes for the season. Keep in mind that many seasonal workers are far from home, so offering them a home-cooked meal and cultivating personal relationships with them could increase the chance that they'll return to work for you the following year.

Another way to identify repeat seasonal workers is through referrals —many temporary workers come from the same locales and know other repeat visitors. They tend to have their own subculture of traveling workers, and often share information about places to work. Just like any other small community, word travels fast among temporary workers. If you treat them well, with the awareness that they are a necessary component of your business, you'll likely have a greater pool of capable workers from which to choose. And if you really want to encourage referrals, offer employees a bonus for anyone you hire through their referral.

Temp Workers and Temp Agencies

Temporary employees are regular employees, even if everyone knows the job will only last a few months. This means you have all the same legal obligations as you would with year-round employees. If you are hiring seasonal workers, you need to be clear with them that the job will come to an end, perhaps even signing an agreement with them to that effect. If you are hiring seasonal workers through a temp agency, they might be considered employees of the agency, of your business, or both, depending on what responsibilities your business and the agency take on with respect to the employee. You may have to pay more to go through a temp agency, but often the agency will do payroll, paperwork, screening, and so on, for you. If the agency takes on enough responsibilities to be considered the sole employer, your potential for liability is lessened (although this situation would likely only be the case for more highly skilled workers).

Hiring and Keeping a Year-Round Staff

While transient workers offer many advantages to a business in paradise, it is virtually impossible for any business to survive on transient workers alone. Even the Whistler community, heavily reliant on temporary workers, has two shoulder seasons between the peak winter and summer months when the number of tourists dries up and the transient workers go home. While some businesses shut down during those shoulder seasons, most stay open. And it is the year-round workforce that will generally carry a business during those off seasons. Additionally, a locally-sourced, well-trained workforce brings consistency and skill to workplaces year-round, and can be valuable trainers and mentors for the transient staff.

Hiring local residents also helps build community relations—everybody knows everybody in a small community, and people appreciate businesses that make an effort to hire their friends, relatives, sons, and daughters. Local staff can also be a valuable source for generating client referrals and potential business partnerships. The permanent staff will likely be the source of most managerial candidates as well. Finding, training, and retaining these workers is crucial if you hope to expand your business (especially if you plan to have more than one location), or increase its value.

Finding and Training Year-Round Workers

Finding year-round workers can sometimes be a challenge in a resort community, especially for a new business. One natural solution is to use a local employment agency, such as Whistler's Personnel Solutions. But many smaller resort areas don't have employment agencies, or you may want to avoid the added cost of using an agency by conducting your own search. See "Start Locally When Hiring Workers—Then Expand Your Territory," above, for some places to begin your search. Of the resources listed there, especially consider members of the senior community, who may be especially valuable as year-round employees. Most resort areas have larger-than-average populations of seniors, many of whom have accumulated years of experience in managing employees, working with customers and clients, and even running businesses. Many seniors enjoy putting some of this experience to work, and while they may prefer part-time shifts, they are often available year-round. Keep in mind that others are dreaming about paradise, too, so if you are looking for someone with a specific skills set, post your job offering in cities where you are likely to find those people. If your business is in Whistler, for instance, post your open position on Vancouver job sites; if your business is in Lake Tahoe, post it on www.craigslist.org in San Francisco. You may find that there are people in larger towns who would jump at the chance to move to your community for the right job.

Remember that these year-round employees will be the core of your workforce, so train them well. They are likely to become managers for at least part of the year when your seasonal workers arrive, so their training should include not only the ins and outs of your business, but training on management responsibilities as well (see "Find Out More," below). For example, they should know what it means to be culturally sensitive, what constitutes sexual harassment, how they can be fair to all workers, and how to motivate them. Also, as discussed later in Chapter 10, you'll need to train them on your firm's unique value proposition—what sets your business apart from others—and your ideal target client.

FIND OUT MORE

If you will be managing employees (and if they will be managing employees), you may want to check out *The Manager's Legal Handbook*, by Lisa Guerin and Amy DelPo (Nolo), for quick answers to questions about dealing with employees. You might also visit the website for the Society of Human Resource Management (www.shrm.org)—although geared more toward human resources professionals and requiring a membership fee, the cost (currently $160, less for non-U.S. members) is not unreasonable for the wealth of human resources material available on its site.

Retaining Employees

As mentioned earlier, the mindset of workers in paradise tends to differ widely from city workers, and that goes for permanent as well as transient employees. It's not that people are so fundamentally different, it's that they change when they arrive in paradise—the smell of the salt air from the ocean or the scent of pine from the forest tends to make work seem less important.

Motivating your year-round employees, therefore, takes on new forms in paradise. Author Chester Elton, whose "carrot" books, such as *The Carrot Principle* (Simon & Schuster), with coauthor Adrian Gostick, have become national bestsellers and who tours the country giving lectures to executives about how to motivate employees, says there is no single best "carrot" that will motivate all workers. The right carrot differs for every company, every department, and often for every worker. The key is learning what drives your employees, what their interests are, and rewarding them accordingly.

While year-round employees seek benefits such as health care and retirement plans, workers who live in paradise locations are also likely to care about their immediate lifestyle. In paradise, a motivating "carrot" may be a season pass to a ski resort, or a day on a fishing charter or in a hot-air balloon.

"Being able to positively impact the people who work for me, and help them all have great lives, is probably the most rewarding part of our business," says Jan Peterson, founder and owner of Jan's Mountain Sports in Park City, Utah (see Chapters 8 and 11 for more about Jan's Mountain Sports).

Every year, and sometimes several times a year, Jan rewards his employees—both year-round and repeat seasonal workers—by taking a group of them on a major fishing trip to some remote part of the globe. Last year, they went to British Columbia. In past years, they have traveled to the Bahamas, New Zealand, Alaska, and Mexico's Yucatán Peninsula. These trips are not all play—Jan also takes customers along on the adventures, and they pay for their own expenses and airfare. But Jan's Mountain Sports covers the employees' expenses, and the trips are memorable experiences that employees look forward to every year. The result has been a low turnover rate at Jan's, and a workforce that has grown consistently as Jan's has grown—from a single shop in 1980 to ten retail locations currently, with 175 workers in winter and 60 in summer.

"Hire the best people, train them completely, and pay them adequately," Peterson opines. "One well-trained professional can do the work of a handful of clerks."

As Cathy Goddard of Whistler's Personnel Solutions notes, "Resort employers have to be very creative in keeping their employees happy." Jan certainly has been creative, but fishing trips are not the only means of attracting and retaining top talent. Rewarding workers with what matters to them can be much more motivational than a $500 bonus at Christmas time. Aside from vacations and resort benefits, flexible hours, family health benefits, the ability to work from home, and time out during the day to allow employees to pick up kids from school are all examples of how resort businesses cater to the needs of their employees.

Of course, paying them the right amount of money is also important. As part of your planning, research what is considered appropriate compensation for the work to be done in the area in which you hope to live. Do not assume that permanent workers can be hired for salaries lower than where you now live. The cost of living in some resort towns can be higher than that in many major cities, and the cost of labor can likewise be higher. See "Paradise Isn't Cheap," below. You do not need to overpay your workers, but compensation should be commensurate with the local cost of living and competitive with what other local businesses are paying. (And, of course, you must comply with minimum wage laws, unless your business is exempt—visit the Department of Labor website (www.dol.gov) for a listing of federal and state minimum wage laws, and the types of businesses and work that are exempt.)

One way to motivate year-round employees is to solicit their input and include them in your business decisions. Have them be a part of the hiring and training of temps and seasonal workers—this will also help prevent friction between the two groups because the permanent workers will be able to spot people they'll be able to work with and, if differences arise later, more motivated to work them out.

Paradise Isn't Cheap

Whistler has the most expensive home prices in all of Canada, far outstripping those in Vancouver, the closest major city. In 2006, the median price of a home in Whistler was 1.26 million Canadian dollars (U.S. $1.20 million). Much of that is due to a cap on development that has pushed up the price of existing homes and the few new developments that are allowed each year. However, recognizing a need for affordable housing for employees, the city of Whistler now mandates construction of affordable housing units as part of the approval of new developments. Rentals are still scarce—for many seasonal workers, the only affordable alternative is to rent rooms in the homes of Whistler residents—and the resulting high housing costs inevitably drive up wages.

Whether your workers are temporary or year-round, screen them well: There's an anonymous quote on the website of Whistler's Personnel Solutions that reads: "The best thing you can do for your competition is to hire poorly." That's not far from the truth. New employees should not only be screened for work history and references, but should also have the personalities and work ethic to match the culture of your business. Finding the right fit with all of your employees, no matter how long they work for you, will make your life much easier as a manager, and bolster your bottom line. ●

Marketing and Promoting Your Business in Paradise

M arketing and promoting a business is an art form no matter where it's practiced. For a small business in paradise, successful marketing and promotion is much like it is in any environment but with some important distinctions. For example, in comparison with a metropolitan area, the customer base in paradise locations is likely to be smaller, so accurately targeting your likely audience is especially important; word-of-mouth referrals and community involvement will likely play a larger role in bringing in new business; the choice of marketing platforms will be narrower; and finding the right help—in the form of agencies or freelance marketing specialists—to develop your marketing plan is likely to be more difficult.

This chapter will walk you through the steps of creating an effective marketing and promotional campaign, and provide help in tailoring that plan to a resort or small-town setting. You will be introduced to three main elements of an effective marketing plan—designing an overall marketing plan and strategy, building public relations, and planning and implementing a successful referral program. A fourth element—community relations and event planning—is essential for the other three to work together successfully. This fourth element is generally much more important to the marketing and promotional process in a resort atmosphere than it is in other, more urban locales, which is why all of Chapter 11 is dedicated to the topic.

About Marketing and Sales

While an effective marketing plan will likely increase immediate sales, it also can—and should—take a longer view by getting the right message to the clients you are seeking, thereby paving the way for future growth. Marketing is therefore not simply sales to a broader audience, but a means of increasing the value of the business. The proprietor of a small business in paradise can accomplish several tasks with an effective marketing plan, including:

- **Promoting the business to a broader base of prospects.** For example, as part of their marketing plans, bed and breakfast owners in Chapter 2, promote their inns on the Internet—not just on B&B sites but on local business and tourist-related sites (such as those related to Cape Cod whale watching).

- **Generating referrals and sales leads.** Ginger Carlson, the Kauai restaurant owner in Chapter 5, increased business for her restaurant by marketing her catering business and collateral products (her line of jams and chutneys).

- **Educating prospects and current clients about your business, informing them about your firm's value, and increasing client retention.** For example, the wine industry creates wine clubs and cooperative marketing organizations—such as those used by the three wineries profiled in Chapter 3—to educate prospective clients and keep existing clients interested in their wineries.

- **Building your firm's brand identity.** Richard Pratt and Cecily Denson from Chapter 2 differentiated their B&B from the multitude of others on Cape Cod by altering its style and marketing it as a classier, posh alternative to the typical country-style B&B.

- **Generating exposure to potential business partners.** Photographer Keoki Flagg from Chapter 5 used a barter system to market his work and his gallery throughout the Lake Tahoe area, and in the process built business partnerships with restaurants, ski resorts, and sports shops.

Crafting Your Marketing Plan

In a paradise setting, it may be tempting to simply let business come to you. After all, part of the lure of living and working in paradise is not having to do all the heavy lifting. And in a small town, everything gets around by word of mouth anyway, right? Unfortunately, building a successful business—even in paradise—doesn't work that way. While word does travel fast in a small community, a strategic, disciplined marketing plan helps ensure the word being spread is the message you want to send. That message can mean the difference not only in the number of clients you attract, but the price point at which you'll be able to sell your goods or services.

A SMALL BUSINESS IN Paradise

To learn more about Switchback Public Relations, visit www. switchbackpr.com.

Brinn Wellise agrees. Brinn is the owner and founder of Switchback Public Relations, an agency located in the Lake Tahoe region that specializes in marketing and public relations for resort-area businesses. For the past eight years, Switchback has led marketing initiatives for ski resorts, restaurant chains, major charity events, retailers, and area chambers of commerce, to name a few. Switchback is itself a small business in paradise, and Brinn has used her own strategies to build a base of solid clients and increase the brand recognition of her own firm. From a one-person shop, Switchback has grown to seven full-time employees and operates out of offices in Truckee, California, a half-hour drive northwest of the lake.

Brinn herself gave up city life and a job at a major marketing agency in San Francisco in favor of the quality of life in Lake Tahoe. She's an avid skier, and in summer likes to go river rafting and mountain biking.

"I came up here to spend a summer with six girlfriends from college, and I just stayed," she said. "That happens a lot in Lake Tahoe."

What's Brinn's advice for promoting your small business in paradise? She offers up what she considers most important in creating a plan, and also some specific marketing activities she finds most effective with her clients. The first five below will be discussed more in this chapter and the last two—creating advisory boards and community involvement—will be discussed further in Chapter 11.

- The most important thing is to understand your target audience, no matter who you are and where you are located.
- Know what gives your business its competitive advantage.
- Do your market research and competitive analysis before getting started.
- Conduct client research—surveys are a great way to measure what works and what doesn't.
- Don't focus solely on the local market. National marketing—or marketing to other cities that have direct flights into the area—can bring in substantial numbers of new clients, especially if your business is in any way related to the tourist industry.
- Form your own advisory board with people you know are well-connected in the community.
- Get involved with local events and charities.

Describe Your Objective(s)

The first step in creating a marketing plan is to assemble a list of objectives. Ask yourself what you are hoping the plan will do for your business. If you are new in town, your primary objective may be to introduce the business's goods and services to the community. Alternatively, you may be trying to position your firm in a certain light, such as the "friendliest bookstore in town." Your objective may be to create a niche business, or target a specific group of potential clients. Similarly, you may want to broaden your existing client base. Client retention or education are other objectives that may be served by a marketing plan. Once you have nailed down your objectives, whatever they are, you can then define the population you are trying to reach.

Define Your Target Audience

As Brinn points out, one of the first and most important steps in creating your marketing plan is to identify and understand your target audience. Who is your typical client? If you have more than one type of clientele, your marketing plan may consider each differently. For instance, a gift store will want to attract walk-in customers, but also market itself to other businesses as a source of business gifts. There may also be a subset of your customers that especially values your goods or services, and to whom you would like to direct your focus. For instance, Ginger Carlson, owner of Caffe Coco and described in Chapter 5, started a catering business to increase the income from her restaurant. Within her catering clientele, she began specializing in catering to Hollywood film crews doing business on Kauai in the off season. Think about your own business: Is there a particular group of customers you would like to attract?

Craft Your Message

Once you know your target audience, you'll need to craft the message you want to send to it. Start by defining your unique value proposition—ask yourself why a customer would prefer buying a product or service from you instead of your competitors. Your message should easily get across what makes your business distinct from the others. Additionally, it should be reflected in every aspect of the business, from the appearance of the business to the attitude of the staff, the details of the service, and so on. For instance, a restaurant trying to convey the message that families are its top priority should have a family-style atmosphere, a kids' menu, crayons or other available amusements, plenty of high chairs, and a no-smoking policy. If you're just getting started in paradise, your message, either through your slogan or what is reflected in the image of your workplace, will be the first impression the community has of your business. Take the time to get it right. Remember to keep it simple—your message should be easy to remember. And keep in mind that once you start getting your message out into the community, you'll have to live up to the promise it offers.

FIND OUT MORE

If you are interested in how to market your business through word of mouth and without the expense of an advertising campaign, you may want to read *Marketing Without Advertising,* by Michael Phillips and Salli Rasberry (Nolo).

Develop Your Strategy

Once you've come up with the message you want to send, the next step is planning how to get that message to the target audience. Write down all the ways you could reach this group. For instance, if marketing to tourists in an area, consider whether there are publications they may read, such as a visitors' magazine provided in local hotel rooms, or a stretch of road they will likely use when driving to or through the region. What events do they attend? What type of new event might they attend? For marketing to local residents, pay attention to where they congregate, such as a local supermarket, sporting good store, watering hole, church, or community meeting place. What local radio and television stations do they listen to or watch? Do they tend to get information from the Internet, and if so, is there a locally oriented website they frequently visit? Additionally, keep in mind Brinn's advice about not limiting your marketing plan to a local audience. Consider how to market your business to tourists that visit your community from other places. When you are traveling, start keeping track of strategies other businesses in paradise use to attract business and build their identities and reputations. Brainstorm with your friends and family— you may be surprised what ideas they have to add.

At this stage in creating your marketing plan, do not consider cost or time—write down all ideas for reaching your desired audience, even if they seem improbable, too expensive, or time-consuming (you never know when the right marketing opportunity will present itself). Once you have a list of ideas, however, carefully examine your resources in terms of time and money—commodities that are limited even in paradise. Where will those funds be best spent to get the right message to the desired customers? One way to choose how to spend your marketing buck is to ask what would most motivate your target client. For instance, if a seafood restaurant is targeting value-conscious families as customers, its marketing strategy would likely be served with coupons, discount nights, or an "under-five-eats-for-free" campaign. On the other hand, a high-end restaurant might prefer to partner with a limousine service or hotel to promote a "romantic weekend" special.

Another important decision in developing your strategy is determining who in your business will be in charge of implementing and monitoring it. Whoever that person is, make sure they don't operate on an island—develop a culture of marketing at your firm. Every person who works for you should be educated on who your ideal client is and what your message—or unique value proposition—is, and should be prepared to discuss them whenever given the opportunity. If you establish a regular process in your company to develop and review marketing strategy, you are more likely to consistently deliver your business message to the right people at the right time, and at the right frequency (which may be especially important in a seasonal business). The right frequency means not oversaturating the market, but making sure your current and future clients see your name and hear your message enough that it sticks.

Evaluate, Evaluate, Evaluate

Once your strategy has been implemented, keep evaluating its effectiveness and how it could be improved. Try as much as possible to determine whether one marketing tool, such as an ad series in the local paper, brought in more customers than another, such as sponsoring a local Little League or Pop Warner team. Evaluate whether the time and money involved with one strategy might be better used with another. For instance, dollars may be better spent on developing a new website for your business rather than purchasing advertising space on another website. Alternatively, perhaps an email newsletter would be more effective than a website.

Most important to evaluate: Are your clients and prospects hearing the message you wanted them to hear? Ask them! Take Brinn's advice and survey your customers and would-be customers to see if they understand the message your business is sending—and whether it matters to them. Sometimes your most important message can get lost within the context of a broad marketing plan. Remember that rarely does anyone develop and deliver the perfect marketing plan right out of the gate, so this portion of your marketing plan is crucial.

Sound like a lot of work? It can be, which is why hiring an outside marketing agency, advertising firm and/or public relations agency can be an effective tool for a small business in paradise. While it will cost some money, an effective plan should be worth the expense in terms of the added exposure (and new customers) it brings your business. Marketing help may be especially valuable if you're new to the area and aren't yet familiar with your customer base and the local media. Of course, the best way to find competent help in a small community is by word of mouth—ask around and see who you can find. Area chambers of commerce and business and community clubs, such as the Rotary Club, can also be good resources.

Building Public Relations

A powerful and often cost-effective means to market yourself and your business is through the creation and implementation of a strategic public relations campaign. Executed wisely, a media campaign can turn a little-known business into the "go-to" place for any given product or service, and can be especially valuable for new businesses not yet known to a community. Effective public relations builds and strengthens your business's reputation by featuring your company's name in newspapers, magazines, books, guides, television and radio programs, websites, and other forms of mass communication. As the owner of the business, and its likely spokesperson, your name and face may get some media time, too. The great thing about it is it's usually free!

Generally, there are three ways you and your business can gain positive media attention. The first, and often the most effective, is in a feature story specifically about you, your company, or its product or service. This is usually the hardest type of news coverage to generate, and often takes time to develop your story, cultivate relationships with journalists, and craft effective press releases that may inspire such coverage.

The second route to media exposure is to be quoted or featured as an expert on a given topic or event. While this may seem to have less of an impact than a feature story about your firm, it may actually reach a wider audience, and can build your credibility and expertise. This type of exposure isn't just for CPAs, lawyers, and stockbrokers. If you sell snowboards, for instance, you can be featured as an expert on the best places in the region to board or the best way to slice a half-pipe. If you rent sailboats, you can discuss local weather and wave patterns. Restaurant and B&B owners are often quoted in travel articles and guidebooks as authorities on local events and culture.

Publicity Online

If you are interested in learning how to use blogs to market your business, browse www.businessblogconsulting.com for insight on creating effective blogs and reaching out to existing and prospective customers. Another blogging resource is Google's Blogger publishing tool (www.blogger.com), which allows you to set up a blog for free.

A third path to media attention is through what could be referred to as the "accidental mention"—you or your firm are featured on television or in a newspaper simply because you happened to be in the right place at the right time. Of course, there are ways to improve your chances of getting accidentally mentioned. You may attend an event that was being featured on the news—and make yourself available to be interviewed about it. You may be at a conference, and give your opinion about the speakers to a local reporter. Whenever you have such opportunities, make sure to give your firm name and location—reporters usually like to describe people as "Bob Smith of ABC Accounting in Pebble Beach."

Generating media attention through the first two means—feature stories and being quoted as an expert—depend on developing good news judgment (recognizing when you or your business has something important to say about a given topic), a good story, and building relations with the press. The third means—the "accidental mention"—depends on your level of moxie and the ability to act quickly.

What Makes a Good Story?

Of course, all of us would like to believe that we should be on the cover of *Time* magazine or *Business Week*. Unfortunately, convincing a journalist of that is not an easy task, but happily you do not need national press to make your small business in paradise a success. To understand what story would look attractive to a reporter, think about the reader or viewer of that reporter's media, whether it is television, radio, a newspaper, a magazine, or the Internet. Exploit any angles that might be appealing to a local newspaper or television station—for instance, Ginger Carlson of Caffe Coco could underline her use of Kauai-produced ingredients in the dishes her restaurant produces. There may be something about your products, building, staff, or yourself that is unusual or connected with other news items as well. For instance, if forest fires are a threat, and you own a hardware store, consider pitching a story about the use or sale of fire extinguishers and shovels. Community events and planning are discussed more fully in the next chapter, but know that any events you sponsor offer a lot of opportunity for publicity. The fact or purpose of the event itself may be newsworthy, or one of the speakers or attendees may be a celebrity or have his or her own interesting story. If so, put together a press release about it and send it to local media.

Working With Reporters

If a reporter—or the author of a book called *Small Business in Paradise!*—happens to call you for your opinion on a given topic—make yourself available as much and as promptly as possible. Remember that reporters are on deadlines. Even if the story isn't timely, they may need to finish it quickly to meet a "news hole" for that day, and if you put your call off until tomorrow, they may end up featuring your competitor instead. Don't insist on seeing the article before it's printed—they will not agree—although you can offer to review factual aspects if the reporter chooses. Keep in mind that the article is their property—and once you've given them a quote, you no longer have control over it. Finally, don't send reporters gifts or try to influence their decision to write about your firm—while the rare reporter can be bought, the wide majority resent any attempt to win them over.

The Press Release

How do you get your story out to the media? Sometimes a brief phone call is appropriate, especially in a casual small-town setting where the purpose of the call is to offer your expertise about a topic in the news, or to alert a journalist to a possibly newsworthy event. Reporters appreciate these "heads-up" phone calls as they help them with their work, but be careful not to sound self-serving. Don't make a call just to alert them to "your story."

While phone calls are sometimes appropriate, press releases are traditionally used to disseminate a story to journalists—they are typically written in news fashion (described more below) and can be easily converted to an actual news story. It makes sense to write a press release about the opening of your firm, a merger or significant new hiring, a new product or service being offered, an event you or your business is sponsoring, or a new way you are supporting a local charity. Writing a press release in "news fashion" requires that the most important details are described first. The release should emphasize those aspects of the story that are unique and have the broadest appeal. Say, for example, that you own a French restaurant and are planning an event for Bastille Day—while the French community may be interested, a newspaper is more likely to carry the story if it focuses on the aspects of the event that appeal to the broader public, such as that you are planning on putting on a fireworks display or giving away free French pastries. Try to keep the length to one page, two pages at most. Put the story into perspective for local journalists, and make sure to list sources and attribution for the facts in the press release. To illustrate some of these pointers, consider this opening paragraph of a press release about a market opening:

Looking for a place to buy fresh fish at reasonable prices? Gail's Fresh Fish announced its grand opening on Route 1 in Marathon Key.

The text might be entirely appropriate for an advertisement, but it is clearly self-serving and offers no incentive for a reporter to write a story about it.

Here's how the opening could be improved:

The first-ever shop on the Keys to feature only locally caught fresh fish and seafood opened today on Route 1 on Marathon Key. Gail's Fresh Fish sells everything from shark and tuna to sea scallops and eel, all of it caught the same day by local fishermen.

This version puts the story into perspective—"the first-ever shop on the Keys"—and offers a timely angle—"opened today"—giving reporters a reason to write the story. Additionally, it offers a local angle—all of the seafood is caught by local fishermen—that makes it appealing to a local reporter. Mentioning shark and eel adds interest and gives a good reporter an idea for a photo shoot. Best of all, it underscores Gail's unique value proposition—the restaurant offers a wide variety of seafood caught fresh that same day.

Know the Media

No matter how interesting your story is, and how well you craft your press release, nothing will happen if you don't get that information to the right people. Find out if there's a press list you can purchase from a local chamber of commerce or from a business associate. If not, put your own list together. Assemble a list of the media organizations in your area, get copies of all of their publications or programs, and find out which journalists are assigned to different "beats." Often it is appropriate to send the same press release to more than one journalist at a publication or broadcast station. The press release about Gail's Fresh Fish, for example, might be of interest to a business reporter, a local news reporter, and even a sports writer or announcer. Note that most local papers employ another person who compiles a calendar section of local events, so if you have even a small event to publicize, he or she would be happy to receive the information.

Promoting yourself and your business may seem daunting when you are a stranger in a new community. Remember that building contacts with the media and establishing your business's reputation in the community is a long-term process, rather than a one-time "splash." Your initial feelings of being an outsider will gradually evolve into feeling accepted, then you'll experience being welcomed as "one of their own," especially if you are successful!

Generating Referrals

Marketing, public relations, and events can all help generate sales leads and improve client retention. However, referrals account for most new clients for small businesses, especially in small-town, resort settings where word of mouth is the best way to spread news, and where community is all-important. Referrals are also inexpensive—your loyal customers are doing most of the work—yet most businesses have no mechanism in place for generating them.

Brinn, from Switchback Public Relations, estimates that "95% of my new business is from client referrals. Lake Tahoe is a tight-knit place. It's all about who you know." That's why she makes it a point to remind her clients about her unique value proposition, and her ideal client profile, and to encourage them to spread the word.

Existing clients and customers are far and away the biggest potential source for referrals, and every small business in paradise should have an established policy to ask clients for referrals, follow up with those referrals, track your success with them, and reward the referring client.

To set up a referral program, start by going through your client list and prioritizing which clients are most likely to generate referrals. Many major corporations today use something called a Net Promoter Score (from *The Ultimate Question* by Fred Reichheld (Harvard Business School Publishing)) to gauge how many of their clients are not only happy, but would happily refer their firm to others. In a nutshell, it adds up how many of your clients are "raving fans" who would refer your business to someone they know, and subtracts from that the number of your clients who are "detractors" and would give you a negative reference. Small companies can institute a similar practice to determine which clients are likely to refer others to their businesses. Since people tend to socialize with people who are like them, your ideal clients (those who are satisfied and loyal) will generally refer your business to ideal prospects. Make sure to follow up by thanking clients for their referrals, and consider offering a discount or other reward for bringing in a new client or customer. Then track those referrals so you know where they came from, which prospective clients to follow up with, and whether your referral program is successful.

Explain any referral program you develop to your employees, and emphasize the importance of telling customers about it. While any program should not be too invasive—you don't want to scare off your best customers!—you can at the least create a brochure or catalogue for your business and ask them to share it with interested friends or business associates. Additionally, let them know about your website—if it is an interesting and helpful one, your clients may refer it to people like them.

Just What Are They Saying?

If your business is travel or resort related, find out what customers are saying. Forums like TripAdvisor (www.tripadvisor.com) rank businesses based on customer's comments, which can be great marketing if the comments are positive. Stay on top of customer responses so that you can fix any problems they raise. If your business is geared toward tourists, you will also want to make efforts to get into travel guides published by various companies, such as the Frommer's and Fodor's guides.

Your referral program should also include a way to track and follow up with any referrals your customers make. You can invest in sophisticated contact management software or use online programs such as www.salesforce.com to manage your referrals. However, if you are not in sales and don't need to manage dozens (or hundreds) of contacts, you can probably track all of your business referrals on standard spreadsheet programs such as Microsoft *Excel*. Doing so will help you keep track of where you are at any given point in time with any prospective client or customer, so you'll know when to follow up without making embarrassing repeat phone calls.

Referrals can also come from sources other than customers, including business partners, trade associations, even the waiter at a local restaurant. That's why networking is of such vital importance in a resort setting, and is the subject of the next chapter—how to integrate your small business in paradise into your new community. ●

Get Involved With the Community

Small towns and resort areas usually offer a sense of community, a general feeling that the residents are all united by a common bond, perhaps because they feel fortunate to share, and obligated to protect, the slice of paradise that they call home. Small business owners in paradise—at least the successful ones—understand the role that community involvement plays in their livelihood. Businesses that support the community will feel that support in return.

For some entrepreneurs, the desire to get more involved in local affairs is one reason they seek a paradise location. As part of what is usually a smaller community, these individuals know that they might have the power to affect and improve their surroundings, and look forward to that opportunity. For other individuals—those who may be more introverted or are simply seeking some peace and quiet—the notion of getting involved in a new community, with the required networking that brings, can seem unappealing, or even downright unpleasant. If you are one of the latter group, and the appeal of moving to paradise in the first place is in "getting away from it all" and enjoying some solitude, you must be thinking, "Why would I ever choose to go out and network?"

Whether you enjoy it or not, networking is a crucial component of success for a small business in paradise. In a small town, networking is by far the best way to make contacts that can develop into business partnerships, supplier relationships, and customers. Getting to know the other members of the community helps get the word out about your business, especially if you are new in town, and cultivating local relationships will help fill in the revenue gaps most seasonal businesses experience every year. In other words, tourists come and go, but local customers are year-round.

Community involvement helps a new business owner do the networking he or she needs to do, and in that regard is more than just a nice-to-do piece of your marketing plan as it may be in a larger community. Instead, it's an essential part of the long-term strategy of any business owner who wants to build, grow, and thrive in paradise. If you hate to network—and the artificiality that implies—becoming a supporter of a local charity or promoter of a community cause can be a personally rewarding way to do something you believe in, while simultaneously making connections for your business. However, avoid causes and connections you do not care about, as your disinterest will eventually show, and you may end up alienating other supporters. Various suggestions will be made throughout this chapter about ways to get involved, but see "How Would You Like to Help?" below, to get your imagination going.

How Would You Like to Help?

Even if you do not think of yourself as a "community person," there are many ways to get involved. Just think about what interests you now, or an activity you used to enjoy but no longer had time for in your busy life. Whatever you choose to do will put you in contact with your fellow residents. Some ideas to get you started:

- Help out at the local humane society
- Collect groceries for a local food bank
- Volunteer at the public library
- Drive for Meals on Wheels
- Be a Big Brother or Big Sister
- Coach a team
- Be a patron of the arts
- Be a Boy Scout or Girl Scout leader
- Volunteer for environmental clean-up
- Join a walk-a-thon.

You can also get ideas by visiting www.networkforgood.org. Check "Volunteer" and type in some key words and your zip code to find local organizations that are of interest to you and need your help.

If done from genuine interest and in a way that promotes and builds partnerships, community involvement can help reduce your business risk. When you have shown your commitment to the place you live, others are more likely to support your business or help you out when you need it. Perhaps Keoki Flagg, profiled in Chapter 5, said it best: "Every time I hit a wall or an obstacle, somebody in the community stepped up and solved it for me." That support was due to the partnerships he developed with other local businesses.

Conversely, if you are someone who loves networking in all its forms, and can't wait to dig into community business, tread a bit carefully. In your excitement about building partnerships and involving yourself in community affairs, you might inadvertently step on some toes. People are the same everywhere, and just as some people might protect their corner offices in the city, others in small towns may fiercely protect their committee membership or their leadership on a given issue. It's important not to appear as if you're sweeping into town and grabbing power, or to imply that you have the answers to all of the problems. In fact, if you're new to town, you probably don't have all the answers, and can learn a lot just by being a silent supporter. Respectful assistance and tact are especially important when getting started, especially in a smalltown.

This chapter will outline some of the most effective ways to get involved with the community. But first, we'll profile a business owner who built a thriving business on many of those "best practices" in community participation.

From Ski Shop Owner to Community Leader

Jan Peterson (mentioned in Chapters 8 and 9), and his wife, Amanda, are model—and essential—members of the Park City, Utah, community. Jan has been a board member of just about every local organization you can name—the Rotary Club, redevelopment committees, and youth organizations, among others. For years, Amanda was chairman of the Park City Chamber of Commerce, organized local mothers to improve the school system, and helped raise funds for local charities.

Jan credits their community involvement as the key to the success of Jan's Mountain Outfitters, the sporting goods retailer he founded in 1980. He believes it is "one of the most important things you can do" when you start a small business in a resort town.

Jan grew up in the sporting goods and skiing business—his father opened the first ski shop in Utah in 1938 and was an instructor for the U.S. Army's famed 10th Mountain Division, a unit specializing in winter and mountain warfare and first activated in World War II. In high school, Jan worked for a sporting goods shop—stringing tennis rackets, mounting ski bindings, repairing trophies, and so on. When it came time for college, however, Jan decided to try a different path. He studied advertising at the University of Utah and, after graduation, spent eight years working at a Salt Lake City advertising agency. Jan grew frustrated with the corporate ad culture and, after one particularly bad day on the job, he phoned his former boss, the owner of the sporting goods shop, who by chance was planning to open a new sporting goods store in Park City. He asked Jan to manage this new store, and it didn't take Jan long to decide to quit his advertising job and move himself, his wife, and two daughters to the resort town outside Salt Lake City.

Eight years later, a car accident put Jan in the hospital, a life-altering event that caused him to again evaluate his life and future. He began toying with the idea of opening his own store, and when a friend offered to invest $25,000 to get him started, his decision was easily made.

Jan's Mountain Outfitters opened its first store in the fall of 1980 and is the largest locally owned sporting goods retailer in Utah, now boasting ten locations. Jan's offers equipment—both for sale and lease— for skiing and winter sports, biking, camping, backpacking, fly fishing, golf, and more. In addition to selling and leasing sporting goods for all of those activities, the business also offers sport outings, events, and instructional camps.

Sporting goods is a relationship business like any other, Jan says, and being engaged in community affairs is the way to establish those relationships. He observes: "The big box stores aren't involved in the community. They come and they take and they leave. The locals understand that."

Why worry about what the locals think? After all, Jan estimates that business from local residents amounts to only about 20% of the stores' business. The other 80% of the customers are "destination people," he says. "But the maitre d' at every restaurant in Park City always gets asked, 'Where should I rent my skis?'" The relationship that Jan's has with the local community often means that the answer to that question is "Jan's."

Get Involved With Charities

Charity work is the first route most people consider when supporting a community, and it is an excellent way to meet local people. While making donations does show your support, devoting some of your personal time and effort gets you connected more quickly, and can be more fulfilling.

Each year, for example, Jan's sponsors a winter sports program called Jan's Winter Welcome, which has raised millions of dollars for children's winter sports programs. While talking with Jan makes it obvious that he derives much personal satisfaction from the program's benefits for children, it's also an extremely important part of Jan's business. In addition to giving his shops instant exposure across the valley and cementing their reputation as community supporters, the program also builds relationships with Park City's future winter sports stars and enthusiasts, many of whom will later become customers and also make referrals.

Jan also serves on the Board of Directors of the National Ability Center, which provides funding for activities for handicapped children. Jan is happy to be involved, but is also clear about the benefits to his business: "It's all about visibility, and showing a willingness to give before you get. People in the community feel comfortable doing business with you because of what you are willing to give."

Build Relationships With Local Companies and Their Employees

Community involvement is not limited to working with local philanthropic organizations, but also includes supporting other members of the business community. Initiating relationships with local business owners and their employees is an important step toward building your local business presence and inspiring loyalty.

Early in the life of the business, Jan's Mountain Outfitters began building relationships with local ski resorts. Jan worked closely with their ski patrols, ski instructors, and employees, helping outfit them for their jobs and often offering employee discounts to win their business. He also joined the board of directors of Ski Utah—a cooperative marketing organization run by 13 major ski resorts in Utah. These relationships paid off—when it came time to award an exclusive contract for a ski shop at the deluxe Deer Valley's Snow Park Lodge, Jan's Mountain Outfitters got the call. That was just the beginning. He now has a location near every major resort in the area, and continues to build strong relationships with all of their employees.

Reaching out to the community also means being selective about where you do your business. Try to support the other businesses in town with your patronage, even if it costs a little more. Business people have long memories, so if you want pizza, eat at the local pizza place that has been doing business there for years. Need an accountant? Don't call the guy who did your books back in the city. Call the CPA in your new community who you met at your son's soccer game, and whose other clients include the mayor and the chief of police!

Once you've established some relationships, consider forming an advisory board comprising some of your best clients and business partners. The objectives of the board are your choice—you can focus on overall business health or on a specific issue you are facing—but should involve advising you on business strategy while also addressing how your business fits into the broader community. The mere creation of such a board shows to the business community that you care about their opinions, and lets clients know you are genuinely interested in meeting their needs, which is likely to generate referrals to their friends and colleagues. Such a group can be of great assistance to you, lending invaluable business advice from widely different perspectives. Of course, this help should be compensated—if you cannot pay your advisory board members, make their participation worthwhile in a different way—put on a monthly dinner for them or offer them a discount at your store. A five-member board is probably sufficient to start with, and you may want more members as time goes on and your business grows. Make it clear that the board is a rotating body, with new appointments made annually so you can bring fresh ideas into the mix, and that it is not a board of directors that will control the business (you and any co-owners are the ultimate decision makers).

Get Involved in Government and Politics

Participation in local politics, and work with governmental and quasi-governmental agencies will also help you and your business gain recognition, as well as offer an opportunity to affect the resolution of local issues. Don't worry—that doesn't mean you should run for mayor. There are plenty of lower levels of government involvement—schools and parks boards and planning commissions, for example, all need individuals to fill their seats, and if you are not in a position to run for those offices, there are usually committees—often staffed by volunteers or appointees—sponsored by each of them. Local redevelopment agencies or government committees formed to seek community input on certain issues are also an excellent way to participate. For instance, Jan's membership on Park City's local redevelopment committees and his work in improving the community's infrastructure helped raise his standing in the community, while also giving him a voice in the improvement of roads and other facilities surrounding Jan's outlets.

This type of work will not only gain exposure for you and your business, but can also have the practical effect of improving your knowledge of local laws and regulations, which may come in handy later. Getting involved in local political campaigns is also a good way to get started on the political scene and to gain exposure to some of the community's movers and shakers (although if your political views run counter to the political views of most of the community, political involvement might not be the best route to promoting your business).

Join Social and Business Clubs

Kiwanis International and the Rotary Club may sound like your parents' organizations, but they are thriving in many small towns across America. Membership extends internationally for many of these organizations, and each has its own mission, usually related to a particular cause or the more general one of organizing local community service. See "Local Groups—Did You Know?" below. One or more of these clubs is likely popular in your town, and joining is one of the best ways to meet fellow local business people.

Local Groups—Did You Know?

Kiwanis International. Founded in 1915 in Detroit, Michigan, this service club targets professional businesspeople as members, and its primary focus is serving the needs of children. See www.kiwanis.org.

Rotary International. Founded in 1905, the organization comprises business leaders and professionals working to provide humanitarian service and promote peace in the world. See www.rotary.org.

Lions Club. Founded in 1917, this organization was formed to assist its members in giving back to their communities through volunteer work. Since Helen Keller spoke at the group's international convention in 1925, however, one of its primary goals is to end preventable blindness. See www.lionsclubs.org.

For all three organizations, you must be invited to join. Check out their websites on the membership procedure, which begins by notifying the organizations of your interest.

Local chapters of these clubs may be found in almost any American—and many international—communities. Additionally, just about every industry has its own organization(s) whose primary purpose is promoting the members' common interests. For example, Michael Talty and David Coffaro are both members of a cooperative wine marketing group called the Russian River Wine Road, organized to help its members build awareness of and market their wines, especially during the slower times of the year. Similarly, bed and breakfast owners Vince Toreno and Patricia Martin are members of a national organization, the Professional Association of Innkeepers International, whose Cape Cod chapter meets periodically to swap ideas and discuss market trends.

State and local chambers of commerce help promote the interests of the business communities in their respective regions. Richard Pratt and Cecily Denson were newcomers to Sandwich, Massachusetts, when they bought their B&B, so they joined the local chamber of commerce, which not only brings together other business and B&B owners for networking events, but also stages events such as Sunday tours of historic homes, which bring both local residents and tourists into their B&B as visitors (and which in turn leads to referrals to new guests). Join the local chamber of commerce as early as possible—you'll meet fellow business owners and learn about local business resources.

FIND OUT MORE

While state and local chambers of commerce support businesses and the business environment in their respective regions, the U.S. Chamber of Commerce represents business interests at the national level on multiple topics, including health care and education (see www.uschamber.com/default). It also offers resources for small businesses at www.uschamber.com/sb.

Many of these organizations—especially those organized around regular meetings—need speakers or presenters. Keep in mind there might be something of interest from your past business or personal experience that would make an interesting talk—and also let people know more about you and your business.

Host and Sponsor Events and Seminars

Event sponsorship is another excellent way to integrate your business into the community while building a clientele. If you're an attorney, for instance, organize and sponsor a free breakfast seminar on a legal topic that is of interest to the community—perhaps probate or real estate law. If you're a restaurateur, participate in the local food and wine fair or "taste of the town" event. If there isn't one, organize it yourself with the help of others. If you're a publisher, sponsor a writing contest. If you cannot think of an event that is clearly related to your type of business, then sponsor an unrelated event.

As part of your overall marketing plan, discussed in more detail in Chapter 10, the first steps in successful event planning is defining your objectives and your target audience. Is your primary objective new business development? If so, you'll want to host an event aimed at developing new business leads and raising awareness of the services you offer. Is your primary objective client retention? If so, your event should focus on building client loyalty and increasing the amount of business your clients do with you.

In paradise, you likely have two distinct types of event attendees— visitors and local residents. If you are targeting tourists during peak season, your event could very well be competing with other events in the community. Keep in mind that most tourists are on vacation —they're likely to have their spouse and possibly their kids along, and they're not going to attend your event unless it sounds like something fun for all of them. If your focus is on local residents and off-season tourists, you may have success with an educational seminar of some type. Your challenge with this audience will be getting the word out to a large enough group of people to make the event a success.

While events can take many forms, most fall into four general categories—educational events and seminars, hospitality events, community events, and firm-specific events. The type of event you organize generally depends on what you want to accomplish and how you want your business to be considered.

Educational Seminars

These events draw in new and existing clients by offering them something of value (information) in exchange for their attendance. Such events are most effective for service firms that need to be recognized as experts in what they do—accountants, lawyers, marketing, and advertising firms. But they can also be useful for other, more consumer-driven businesses looking to set themselves apart from their competition. Jan's hosts backpacking and fly-fishing outings, which raise awareness about a sport and sporting equipment and may generate new business. A restaurant or a gourmet deli might offer a free class on how to match wine with food, which will likely prompt additional sales. An art gallery might offer a lecture about a particular style of art or a seminar on art appreciation. Ask yourself if there is information you know that others would like to learn, and that will be basis for your educational event.

Hospitality Gatherings

These events are meant to simply entertain your guests and their success depends on creating a relaxed atmosphere where you and your invitees can get to know each other. These events work equally well for both existing and prospective clients, as the latter will have an opportunity to meet you and ask other guests how they like working with you. Hospitality events also work well as client referral gatherings—ask your best clients to invite a guest. Done right, they reflect well on your business, express appreciation for your current clients, and show prospective clients the quality of attention they will receive from you. The key to a successful hospitality event is to keep it small enough to create a sense of exclusivity (each person will feel privileged to be invited), and casual enough to support easy networking among the guests. Twenty to 30 people is generally a good number. Holiday parties, themed cocktail hours, golf outings, wine and cheese events, and live music concerts typically fit into the hospitality event category.

Community Events

While likely the most work, community-wide events are probably most effective for generating business recognition and integrating yourself into the local community. Think of the area historic tours in which B&B owners Richard Pratt and Cecily Denson participate. This is not the type of event that you want to do alone. Enlist the support of other businesses and organizations. "Taste of the Town" events, marathons, fairs, and contests are all examples of community events. Linking your event to a local charity is recommended, as that link, while also benefiting the charity, can offer you instant recognition as someone who cares and plans to contribute to the local community. Involving local government agencies or fire and police departments can also be a good idea—in fact, you may need to involve them to get permits for the event anyway. If possible, and appropriate, try to create an event that is clearly linked to the type of business that you do—Jan's Winter Welcome is a good example.

Firm-Specific Events

Some business occasions are geared to introducing your firm to the local community and prospective new clients. These differ from hospitality events because their focus is not on the event's entertainment value, but rather on your business. Grand openings fall under this category, but even professional service-oriented firms that may view official grand openings as too glitzy can hold similar gatherings under a different name. Call the event an open house, or some other name fitting your firm or business. For example, if Richard and Cecily weren't already offering historic tours of their B&B, they could hold a holiday open house, opening their doors to the community so that residents can see what their B&B has to offer. As in any type of event, giveaways of some kind are often recommended, as long as they reflect well on your business.

Tips for Successful Events

- Make sure the event is at a convenient time and a place where your guests will feel comfortable and that reflects well on your firm.
- Don't skimp on food and beverage—make sure there's enough to go around. While an international theme can be fun, consider focusing on local cuisine or showcasing a particular local restaurant, chef, or beverage producer—it shows community support and can help establish ties with local food and beverage providers.
- Limit firm-specific presentations to ten minutes, and educational seminars to less than an hour.
- Allow sufficient time for questions and answers, and plenty of time both before the presentation and after it for casual networking.
- If you are making a luncheon presentation, schedule your talk to begin as dessert is being served.
- Prepare for foul weather. Make sure you have an alternative venue or a means of contacting all your guests if you need to cancel at the last minute.

Don't Just Join ... Lead!

How much you get out of your community work depends in large part on the effort you put into it. You can join the Rotary Club and the Lion's Club, the PTA and the chamber of commerce, and you can show up at a charity at holiday time to bag groceries for the poor. That will help, but if you truly want to build your business in a small town environment, it takes more than just minimal effort. It takes leadership and true concern for the improvement of your community and the betterment of the people in it. If you take initiative in solving a problem or otherwise help out your community, other residents will sit up and take notice. And they won't likely forget! That leadership breeds loyalty, and translates into more business.

In paradise, building relationships can make the difference between a thriving business and one that never gets off the ground. This often comes as a surprise to many a budding entrepreneur, especially those whose motivation for moving out of the city is to find peace and solitude. Not everybody is cut out for the social and community life required to run a successful business in a small resort town. Still, even if you're not "the networking type," you might be surprised to find that you actually enjoy the community involvement that a resort town can offer.

Even in Paradise—An Overview of Legal and Tax Issues

The allure of working in paradise may be partially based on the hope of simplifying your life and eliminating the stresses associated with living in a major metropolitan area—the impossible deadlines, the red tape, the constant bills and taxes, and so on. The "simple life" is not always simple, however. Some people who plant themselves in paradise may be disillusioned when they discover that the delights of bureaucracy—whether related to getting licenses or permits, discovering unexpected deadlines, suffering through some sort of approval process, paying special assessments, or receiving unexpected tax bills—also exist outside the city.

While this may seem surprising, there are several reasons for this complexity. The first is that while you may escape metropolitan red tape, Big Brother is still watching—and you'll still need to deal with U.S. federal, state, and other local laws and regulations (or the laws of another country if you will be doing business outside the United States). In some cases, that can seem doubly hard when you are located somewhere out in the country where state and federal agencies may not have offices. Second, government agencies in smaller communities—and the people who populate them—tend to go along doing what they've been doing, the same way they've been doing it, for years, primarily because there is not much pressure to change it. Big city infrastructures and big city budgets also tend to bring big city efficiencies—the incentive to bring a paper application process online for a business license, for instance, is much greater if 400 people will use it each month, as opposed to four. Those efficiencies may be lacking in a rural or small town setting. As a newcomer, there is little you can do to change the system of doing things. If a local planning department wants to charge $1,000 for a permit to pave your business driveway, and it will take six weeks to complete the approval process, then be prepared to spend $1,000 and wait for six weeks to get the approval you need. Third, there may be unwritten rules or "accepted" ways to do things in a small community that you would not know unless you have also been a long-term resident. This is not to say that small town administrators or government employees are secretive or devious—often the funds are not available to update published community information or long-time practices may be so familiar to the people doing business in a community that there's no perceived need to articulate them.

The best way to deal with the not-so-simple processes and procedures of local governance is to just find out how everybody else does it, and follow suit. If you arrive in a new setting with a preconceived notion about how things ought to be, and try to impose your expectations on the process, you'll only be frustrated and may unwittingly step on some local toes in the process. As the old saying goes, "When in Rome ..." And speaking of Rome, if your small business is in a foreign country, the advice to do things the way the locals do goes double. (See "Hoping to Become an Expatriot?" below, for resources for non-U.S. businesses.) Horst Drechsler, profiled in Chapter 7, says he's watched many foreigners come and go on the Brazilian island where he runs his inn because they just couldn't figure out the "jeitinho." The word "jeitinho" in Brazil is best described as a "little way" of doing things that is decidedly Brazilian. If you embrace it, you can accomplish just about anything you set your mind to do. But if you resist it, getting anything done is going to be a struggle. Learning such customs is one of the first things you'll need to do when setting up shop in a foreign country. Large corporations often hire consultants to train expatriate managers on the business customs of a new country where they are assigned. Small business owners usually don't have that luxury, but you can learn a lot from other local expatriates who have built similar businesses, and from many locals and government officials. Asking a local friend or colleague to walk you through the process of setting up a business will help educate you in the way things are done in the community, and his or her involvement may actually open doors for you. In many less-developed countries, you can often hire a "fixer" to help smooth out some of the bureaucratic red tape. However, be careful to hire someone who comes recommended by someone you trust—otherwise the fixer may end up "fixing" much more than they really need to, just to earn more money.

Hoping to Become an Expatriate?

If you are looking to start a business in a foreign destination, below are some resources to help get you started:

Visit the U.S. Department of Commerce website (www.commerce.gov). The U.S. Department of Commerce has a wealth of information for you as you consider your foreign business venture—and it's free! For taxation rules, and other nitty-gritty aspects of your business, this should be the first stop on your way out of the country.

Choose your own adventure. If you don't have a particular destination in mind, planning for anywhere-but-here can be extremely difficult. So start finding the best locale for your business by using the Library of Congress's "Portals to the World" feature (www.loc.gov/rr/international/portals.html). You can find extensive information about any country you wish, and choose the one that best suits you.

Read up. Use the U.K.'s *Guardian Unlimited* guide to English-language publications throughout the world to catch up on local coverage of the business market you're looking to join (www.guardian.co.uk/worldnewsguide).

Feel out the market. Talk to people in your hoped-for business locale to make sure you've got a good fit—who's going to visit a snowboarding shop in the Bahamas? Finding advisers who are well-versed in the local particulars will be essential, so use your scouting missions described in Chapter 6 to start the all-important networking process. You can start by learning from those who've come before; try www.expatexchange.com, one of the most expansive communities of expatriates on the Internet.

Protect yourself. Not just your life and limb, but your intellectual property as well. Make sure that you're receiving excellent legal advice so that your product will be well-protected in the market, and that any contracts you've signed are legally enforceable. Visit www.workandliveabroad.com for the legal advice collected there, as well as immigration information for many countries.

Hoping to Become an Expatriate?, cont'd.

Consider franchising. America's not the only place where you can start a franchise, and many American franchises would be right at home anywhere in the world. Starbucks in Munich? McDonald's in Beijing? Choose your franchise and market, and make it happen! Start with the International Franchise Association at www.franchise.org.

Some other websites that may be useful:

- The website for the International Labour Organization, an organization promoting decent work worldwide by setting international labor standards: www.ilo.org/public/english/standards/norm.
- A directory for expatriate communities online: www.transitionsabroad.com/listings/living/resources/expatriatewebsites.shtml.
- For tips on global business etiquette: www.executiveplanet.com/index.php?title=Main_Page.
- For guides to help you make your dream job a reality job, see www.fabjob.com/welcome.asp.

The Right Attitude

In seeking paradise, you are likely looking for a new way of doing things in your own life, so try being open to the business requirements and practices in your new locale. You may find local government slower, more cumbersome, or just not what you expected, but if you can relax into it, you'll adapt more quickly to the local way of doing things, and likely make new business associates along the way. If you are moving to a small community, remember also that your appearance in the community will be the subject of curiosity and your first dealings with government officials and local business people will form the basis for your reputation. Every person you meet or work with is a potential customer, neighbor, or social contact, or is related to one, so monitor your behavior and reactions with that in mind. Once you understand that going with the flow of local custom will be more effective than fighting it, and you can approach your new adventure with an open attitude and genuine curiosity, you can move on to understanding and implementing the all-important tax and legal issues that are necessary to running any business, wherever located.

Buying a Business Versus Starting From Scratch

One way to avoid many of the start-up chores related to a new business—as well as the possible surprises and frustrations arising from doing so in an unfamiliar locale—is to buy an existing business (or part of one) instead of starting your own. This approach, followed by Keith Savitz (a co-owner of the East End Café, profiled in Chapter 4), and by Fiona and David Love (owners of Candy & Kites, also described in Chapter 4), can appear less daunting. Presumably, with an existing business, necessary permits and licenses have been obtained, a business structure chosen and documented, and appropriate governmental relationships established. Additionally, many essential business relationships are already in place, including those with customers, employees, suppliers, shipping companies, insurance brokers, and other local business people.

However, the good standing of the business—both legally and with respect to its relationships—is dependent on the prior owner's diligence. If you do buy an existing business, see for yourself whether the seller has taken all the necessary steps to legally conduct his or her business, as well as maintained cordial and profitable business relationships. While you may "piggyback" onto some else's start-up efforts, you will also inherit any problems or difficulties of the existing business.

The details of purchasing a business are too complex to be fully covered here, but if you decide to do so, in general you will need to decide whether to buy the business's assets, or if it is a corporation or LLC, its equity ownership (see "Decide on Your Business Structure," below, for a discussion of the different types of business entities). That decision will affect the contents of any purchase agreement, but whatever route you take, ensure that the seller has taken proper steps to form the business and maintain any corporate housekeeping necessary during the life of the business. For instance, if the business is a corporation, you would investigate whether it is considered in "good standing" in the state, which usually requires that the entity has paid any taxes it owes and filed appropriate reports. If the business has employees, has the owner paid its federal and state employment taxes? Has the owner gotten all permits, both from local, state, and federal authorities (if necessary) to do business? Are any licenses necessary to operate the business transferable to new owners or will you have to acquire a new license if you buy the business?

Buy Your Bliss

There are functional businesses for sale all over the country, and just like apartments or houses, they're listed in the classifieds. Check out the newspaper published in your paradise location, or search through the listings at www.businessesforsale.com or www.businessbroker.net, which together have thousands of listings for all 50 states.

While these are just some of the items to review in a business purchase, a suitable purchase agreement would include a clear delineation about what is being purchased, the purchase price and how it is being paid, a list of the seller's "representations and warranties" about multiple aspects of the business (including its good standing, the quality of the business relationships, whether there are any outstanding lawsuits or other ongoing legal or regulatory problems, whether the business assets being purchased are in good condition, whether there are any liens on the business property, whether licenses and any contracts of the company are transferable to a new owner), and usually an indemnity provision, whereby a seller would promise to repay you for damages resulting from misrepresentation about those items, and an agreement by the seller to do what he or she needs to do after the sale to transfer any licenses or agreements to the business under its new ownership. Even though the seller may agree to an indemnity provision, however, you as a buyer should do your homework before agreeing to purchase any business, and review carefully all documentation related to the enterprise's authority to do business. Additionally, after purchasing a business, make sure to follow up with governmental agencies and other businesses, doing what you need to so that all registrations, licenses, permits, insurance policies, and business agreements reflect you as the business owner.

 FIND OUT MORE

If you would like to learn about purchasing a business, take a look at *The Complete Guide to Buying a Business*, by Fred Steingold (Nolo) (it comes with a CD-ROM with documents you can adapt for use in any purchase, including a purchase agreement). Because local laws and regulations may play a part, it makes sense to enlist the help of someone who is familiar with them to review any purchase agreement and related documentation prior to a purchase of a business. Here is one area where it is usually worth hiring an attorney, and if you can find a local business attorney—usually you find the best ones by word of mouth—all the better (see "Hiring Professional Help" at the end of this chapter).

Decide on Your Business Structure

As earlier mentioned, one advantage of buying an existing business is that the business structure has already been chosen. Still, you'll need to make sure that structure fits your own needs and plans for the future of the business. For example, if it doesn't provide enough flexibility for growth (for instance, the ability to easily take on investors), or enough protection from business liability, or if it is too costly to maintain for the benefits it offers, consider whether a different form of business might be appropriate.

Whether buying an existing business or starting your own, however, one of the most important decisions you'll make is what type of structure you want for your business. As briefly described in "Estimate Your Start-up Costs" in Chapter 6, the four possible structures for small businesses in the United States are sole proprietorships, general partnerships (limited partnerships also exist, but are relatively rare and will not be addressed here), limited liability companies (LLCs), and corporations. The choice in structure may initially seem obvious to you, but you should carefully examine each option's advantages and disadvantages before deciding.

A sole proprietorship (or, if there is more than one owner, a general partnership), is the simplest form of corporate structure and generally inexpensive to establish. These classifications are "default" classifications that apply if concrete action is not taken to form a business entity separate from the owners, which would include filing Articles of Incorporation for a corporation or Articles of Organization for an LLC with the secretary of state's office (or equivalent filing office) in the state in which it is doing business. Therefore, if you are Joe and you open Joe's Bait Emporium—without partners and without setting up a corporation or LLC—your business will be considered a sole proprietorship.

Sole proprietorships and partnerships are not considered to be separate from their owner(s), and therefore do not file separate tax returns or pay corporate taxes. Instead, each owner is taxed on his or her share of the profit from the entity.

The primary disadvantage of these types of business entities is that, because owners are not considered separate from their sole proprietorships or partnerships, owners share the liability of the business. If someone trips in Joe's Bait Emporium and decides to sue, he or she will in effect be suing Joe personally, and all of his assets will be available for any judgment or settlement. While the risk of liability can be lessened with insurance coverage, liability over coverage limits will still be the responsibility of the owner(s). Additionally, insurance coverage cannot be obtained for some business liabilities, such as business debt. The personal liability issue can be even more scary with partnerships—partners are fully liable for their partners' business decisions, even if one partner acts alone. In other words, if your business partner signs a ten-year lease on a property, you are liable personally under the terms of the lease (and for the entire amount of the lease payments, not just your share), even if you did not consent (or know about) the deal.

This potential liability is the primary reason that entrepreneurs choose the LLC or corporation form of business entity. Although not bullet-proof, both protect owners from personal liability for business debts and court judgments against the business. (There are some situations where personal liability is still a risk, such as when owners personally guarantee a third-party loan to the business, which is usually required by financial institutions making small business loans; when owners do not respect the boundaries of the business entity and treat assets of the corporation or LLC as their own; or when an owner intentionally hurts someone or acts illegally or fraudulently.) Additionally, if you plan to seek investors, an LLC or corporation structure will likely be necessary, both for the ease of structuring those investments and because of investors' desire to avoid personal liability as an owner of your business. While more expensive to maintain than sole proprietorships and partnerships (there are usually annual state fees), LLCs and a type of corporation (the S corporation) also offer the advantage of "pass-through" taxation of a sole proprietorship and general partnership; i.e., the business is not taxed separately, and the owners of the entity are taxed on their share of the business's taxable income, while offering liability protection.

In general, LLCs require less "housekeeping" than S corporations and are subject to fewer restrictions in their organization. Among other restrictions, S corporations can only have a certain number (not more than 75) of certain types of shareholders (non-U.S. citizens or residents are precluded, as well as any entity that is not an individual person, such as corporations, LLCs, or partnerships). There are no such restrictions on owners of LLCs (or "members"). S corporations are required to issue stock, hold regular shareholders' and board of directors' meetings and keep minutes of those meetings, among other requirements specified by their specific state's law. LLC members do not need to satisfy those formalities, and can simply agree at the outset on the management of the business. Finally, LLCs offer some flexibility in how profits and losses are allocated among members. While S corporations are required to split profits and losses among its shareholders according to the percentage of stock each shareholder owns, LLC members can agree to a different split of profits and the related tax liability.

While these are some of the general differences among the types of business entities, there is far more to consider in choosing a business structure. See the resources in the next "Find Out More," below, for a more detailed discussion about different types of ownership structures.

Getting Started

If you decide to form a corporation or an LLC, as opposed to a sole proprietorship or a partnership, you will need to register with the state in which you are setting up your business by filing a formal document with the secretary (or department) of state—usually Articles of Incorporation for a corporation and Articles of Organization for an LLC. What this document is actually called and the specific requirements for filing it varies among states, and your secretary of state's office should be able to provide you with the requirements. You can also choose to pay an online service such as The Company Corporation (www.corporate.com) to handle this and other set-up matters.

Choosing a Name for Your Corporation or LLC

As part of this registration process, you will need to choose a name for your corporation or LLC that is not taken by another corporation or LLC in that state. While each state varies in its procedure, you may be able to search your state's database to make sure that the name of your business is not already taken before filing, and in some states you can reserve a name until you file your organization documents with the state. Keep in mind, however, that clearance by the state does not ensure that you aren't violating a trademark—it only verifies that no other business with that name has registered in the corporation or LLC database in that state. To check whether you are infringing on a registered trademark, you'll need to conduct a separate federal trademark search.

Corporate Start-Up Tasks

If you have chosen a corporate form for your business, you have several other important tasks to accomplish in getting started, including electing a first board of directors and holding its first meeting (depending on your state law, you may only need one director if you are the sole shareholder, but you might consider soliciting one or two members of the local community to be on your initial board); adopting bylaws that spell out the rights and powers of shareholders, directors, officers, and other issues; issuing a stock certificate to each shareholder; setting up a corporate bank account; and establishing a corporate record book for important documents.

Additionally, if you are electing to set up an S corporation, you'll need to file with the Internal Revenue Service a completed Form 2553 (*Election by a Small Business Corporation*). This document can be downloaded from www.irs.gov.

LLC and Partnership Start-Up Tasks

After filing registration documents with the state, LLCs do not have to jump through the record-keeping hoops that corporations do. However, if there is more than one member of the LLC, it makes sense to create an agreement among the owners that addresses, at a minimum, management of the company, transfer of ownership, and how profits and losses will be split among the members. Additionally, general partnerships, while not required to file formation documents with the state, will generally benefit from a partnership agreement that outlines each partner's share of ownership, power to make decisions, what will happen if one partner decides to leave the partnership, and so on— otherwise, that state's law will determine how all of those issues will be decided for the partners.

FIND OUT MORE

While choosing a business structure, setting it up, and running it can seem quite daunting, Nolo offers many resources to help you in these tasks. For choosing a business structure and getting started, *Legal Guide to Starting & Running a Small Business,* by Fred Steingold, and *The Small Business Start-Up Kit,* by Peri Pakroo, are helpful. For information about forming and running LLCs, see two titles from Anthony Mancuso: *Form Your Own Limited Liability Company,* and *Your Limited Liability Company: An Operating Manual.* For help meeting state rules for corporate meetings and other corporate housekeeping tasks, take a look at *The Corporate Records Handbook: Meetings, Minutes & Resolutions,* by Anthony Mancuso. For more information about partnerships, see *Form a Partnership: The Complete Legal Guide,* by Ralph Warner and Denis Clifford. Most of these titles have forms on CD-ROM to help you with these tasks. These and other business books and software are available at www. nolo.com, where you'll also find lots of useful and free information on ownership structures and starting a business.

Registrations, Licenses, and Permits

Once you have set up your business, you will likely need to file applications with various government agencies. Four types of registrations or applications are common for businesses operating in the United States: a federal employer identification number application, a local tax registration (often referred to as a business license), a fictitious business name registration, and a resale (or seller's) permit.

Federal Employer Identification Number

Don't be misled by the name—the federal Employer Identification Number (EIN) must be obtained by almost all businesses, whatever their form, and whether or not the business will ever hire employees (with one exception, described below). The EIN is essentially the equivalent of a business's Social Security number, and will be used on just about any document relating to the business, including license and permit applications of all types, tax forms, or nongovernmental documents such as bank loan applications. (The only type of business that does not require an EIN is a sole proprietorship with no employees—the owner may simply use his or her Social Security number.) It's easy to get an EIN—you can file IRS Form SS-4 by mail or online, or get a number over the phone (see instructions at www.irs.gov).

Local Tax Registration

You are more likely to hear this called a "business license" but registration at the local level (the town and/or county in which you are doing business) is usually accompanied by a flat fee or one based on some other factor, such as estimated sales or number of employees.

Fictitious Business Name Registration

Anytime your business operates under a name other than yours (if you are a sole proprietorship), all of the partners' (if a partnership), or the official name contained in the Articles of Incorporation or Articles of Organization filed with the state (for a corporation or LLC), you are required to file a notice—usually with the county (sometimes the state) in which you are doing business. The purpose is to prevent confusion arising from two businesses operating under similar names and also to allow the public to discover the true owners of a business.

Resale License (or Seller's Permit)

If you are planning to sell goods, you will likely need to obtain a seller's permit, usually from the tax or revenue department of the state in which you are doing business. As a requirement of obtaining this permit, you will be obligated to collect sales tax on goods you sell, and periodically submit those payments to the state.

Then There's That Big Pile of "Other" Licenses, Registrations, and Permits

What, there's more? Licenses and permits can be the bane of the small business owner. Sometimes it may seem like there's absolutely nothing you can do or change about your business that doesn't require some form of government license or approval (with an accompanying fee). And yet, complying with what may seem like pointless requirements may be the lesser evil, as avoiding them can result in even more painful experiences down the line.

Say, for example, that you ignore a county planning ordinance that seems to require obtaining a permit for replacing a wall on your business's parking structure. Or maybe you just didn't know that such a permit was required. Regardless, the lack of a permit could prompt the county to order the dismantling of the structure. Even if that didn't happen, the lack of a permit could lower the resale value of the property.

Licenses and permits serve many purposes: protecting public health and safety, preserving the environment and aesthetics of a community, and of course raising money for local, state, and federal governments, to name a few. In general, you may need a license to do a particular type of job (a federal license is necessary to be an investment advisor, for instance, and state licenses usually are required for certain health care workers, legal practitioners, and cosmetologists, to name a few) or to produce or sell particular items (such as drugs and alcohol and for the sale of firearms) or if you work with hazardous material or discharge any materials into the air or water. Local town or county regulations will likely govern where your business is located (zoning), including what type of businesses you may run from home, whether it is a nuisance (noise ordinances, planning commission approvals) or is unsafe (building permits). Depending on your business and where it is located, you may need a sign permit from the city or county planning department, waste discharge permits from the county health department, a license to sell state lottery tickets, or a permit from the county to operate a light manufacturing business. As you can see from this variety, it's hard to know for sure what types of licenses and permits might be required in your community for your type of business. There's also no single source you can tap to find out, but the local government is a good first place to start. You might also check with a state agency governing your type of business to see if they have a checklist for that state's requirements. The local and state chambers of commerce are sometimes good resources as well.

Tax Reporting Basics

If your small business in paradise is the first business you have owned, you'll need to gain a basic understanding of business taxes and the types of returns you will need to file, and more importantly, develop a plan for how to manage your tax filings. If you have a fairly simple business and operate it as a sole proprietorship, you can probably do it all yourself using a combination of a business accounting program such as *QuickBooks*® and tax software such as *TurboTax*.® If you have a partnership, an LLC, or a corporation, or your business is more complicated—for instance, your business is large, complex (perhaps has both a manufacturing and a retailing component), or is eligible to receive tax subsidies, such as in certain farming operations, you'll probably want to hire an accountant, at least to review your tax filings and make sure there's nothing you missed. If your business requires a lot of time with respect to keeping track of inventory or other costs, or you will have employees, you may want to hire not only a tax accountant but also an experienced bookkeeper, at least part time, to properly account for income, costs, and payroll.

In general, there are three main types of business taxes collected at the federal government level: income taxes, employment taxes, and self-employment taxes.

Income Taxes

Each type of business entity reports its income differently. For a sole proprietorship, business income is accounted for on IRS Schedule C and filed along with your federal Form 1040. Your business income (or loss) is added to (or subtracted from) any other income you report on the Form 1040.

For a business organized as a partnership, each partner reports his or her profit or loss from the partnership on IRS Schedule E and files it along with his or her Form 1040. While the partnership pays no taxes on its own behalf, it is nonetheless required to file a Form 1065, an informational tax return telling the IRS each partner's share of the partnership income. (This form is sometimes referred to as a Schedule K-1, because a separate Schedule K-1 listing each partner's share is filed as an attachment to the form.)

An S Corporation, which for tax purposes is a "pass-through" entity and does not pay income tax at the corporate level, is nevertheless required to file an informational tax return, Form 1120-S, with each shareholder filing a Schedule E with his or her personal Form 1040. A C Corporation, considered a separate taxable entity from its shareholders, files either Form 1120 or Form 1120-A and may owe tax on its income.

Unless the owner(s) (or member(s)) of an LLC elect otherwise, an LLC is usually treated for tax purposes like a sole proprietorship if there is only one member, or like a partnership if there are two or more members. If taxed as a sole proprietorship, the owner will include the LLC income or loss on Schedule C and file it as part of his or her regular return. If taxed as a partnership, the LLC will still need to file an informational return, Form 1065, used by partnerships, with each partner including his or her income or loss on Schedule E on his or her regular tax return.

Employment Taxes

If your business has employees, you'll need to pay several types of payroll taxes. To start, you must withhold federal income taxes from your employees' paychecks based on the information each employee provides on their IRS Form W-4 (see "Workplace Laws and Regulations," below), along with the employee's share of Social Security and Medicare, and the Federal Unemployment Tax (FUTA). You'll also have to pay the employer's share of Social Security and Medicare for each employee. Amounts withheld and the employer's share of Social Security and Medicare must be regularly submitted to the federal government. Because of the detail involved and the multiple reports to be filed throughout the year, some business owners choose to hire a bookkeeper or an outside payroll service to take care of all of the withholding and filing requirements.

Self-Employment Taxes

As the owner of a sole proprietorship or a partnership, or the member of an LLC where you are actively involved in the business (although the rules for LLC members are not yet clearly defined), you'll need to pay self-employment tax on your share of the business's income. Self-employment tax is designed to replace the Social Security and Medicare taxes (both the employer's and the employee's shares) that would be paid if you were working as an employee for another company. Self-employment tax is reported each year on IRS Schedule SE and submitted with your Form 1040.

Of course, these are the types of business taxes typically collected by the federal government. Most states also collect taxes on business income and payroll, and as mentioned earlier, most also require that businesses collect, and submit to the state, sales taxes on the sale of tangible goods. There may be other types of state, county, or city taxes—on particular types of goods such as tobacco or alcohol, or on particular industries, such as hotel or tourism taxes, or on particular assets, such as business assets or real property. When you are deciding on a location for your business, consider whether your business will be subjected to taxes that it would not be if located in another area. Before you get too discouraged about taxes, however, remember that many resort areas offer tax breaks and other incentives to new businesses that locate there. Investigate the requirements of these development incentives before investing, however—they may only be available before you set up your business or may be limited to certain types of businesses or those located in certain physical locations in the community.

 FIND OUT MORE

Each business and its owner(s) have different circumstances that determine what tax requirements apply and how taxes are reported and paid. It may make sense to speak with a qualified tax professional before starting your business to make sure that the structure and tax treatment makes sense for your personal situation. Some other resources to help you understand tax law and possible strategies for minimizing tax liabilities include *Tax Savvy for Small Business*, by Frederick W. Daily, and *Deduct It! Lower Your Small Business Taxes*, by Stephen Fishman (Nolo). IRS Publication 334, *Tax Guide for Small Businesses*, also provides a helpful overview for getting started.

Workplace Laws and Regulations

If you already manage employees, you know that hiring an employee triggers a multitude of federal, state, and even local laws regarding reporting and the employment relationship. These are in addition to the payroll withholding and tax payments described above. When hired, every new employee must fill out three forms right away—an IRS Form W-4 (for determining withholding amounts), a Form I-9 (the U.S. Citizenship and Immigration Service's form verifying employment eligibility in the United States), and a new hire reporting form, to be submitted to state and federal child support agencies.

Perhaps more troublesome for employers are the potential liabilities that employees bring, either because of actions by the employee that involve a third party, or because of interactions between the employer and employee. There is no sure-fire way to make sure that the employees you hire won't get you or your company into trouble, although careful hiring, training, adequate supervision, and sufficient insurance will go far in preventing liability to third parties stemming from your employees' actions.

FIND OUT MORE

To avoid legal snafus with the people you interview and hire, check out *The Employer's Legal Handbook*, by Fred Steingold (Nolo). This comprehensive book provides complete details on workplace laws and regulations, from hiring through firing and everything in between —including applicants' privacy rights, background checks, antidiscrimination laws, wage and hour rules, employee benefits, workers' compensation insurance, workplace safety issues, and much more.

Contracts and Legal Disputes

As a business owner, you will be entering into contracts with vendors, customers, and others, perhaps without even recognizing that you have done so. A valid contract requires only two things: an agreement on the major issues between the parties, and "consideration"— a legal term meaning the exchange (or promise) of something of value for something else of value. A contract does not have to be in writing to be legally binding (although each state requires that some contracts be in writing, for instance, those involving real estate). In paradise, many of the people you do business with may be used to oral contracts or handshake agreements. For example, if you hire Joe the contractor to install a hood vent on the stove in your restaurant kitchen, and he promises to have it finished in two weeks for a certain price, you have a legal contract. A breach of that contract by either party is enforceable, provided that the existence of the contract can be proven. That is why it's a good idea to put all important contracts in writing (and get them approved by an attorney, as appropriate). Without a written document, you may be unable to prove that you were in agreement on all the terms or that the agreement existed at all. A good written contract does not have to be lengthy, but should include the following information, as appropriate:

- Names and addresses of the parties
- The date the contract is signed
- A short summary of the background of the agreement
- What each party is promising to do
- When the work will be done or the product delivered
- How long the contract will remain in effect
- The price, or how it will be determined
- When payment is due
- Warranties or guarantees about the work, if any
- Conditions under which each party can terminate the agreement
- Liquidated damages, if appropriate (a fixed amount to be paid if the contract is breached)

- Whether or not the contract is transferable
- Arbitration or mediation of disputes
- Whether or not the party that breaches the contract is responsible for the other's legal fees
- Where notices of default or other communications can be sent
- What state law applies if questions arise.

As sure as the sun rises in the East and sets in the West, there will be instances when your small business gets involved in some sort of dispute (perhaps in connection with one of your contracts). It may be a situation where you feel your business is the injured party, such as when a vendor overcharges you on an order. Or it may be that a guest at your bed and breakfast wants her money back because a neighborhood dog barked all night, keeping her awake. The vast majority of business disagreements can be resolved by simply talking about the situation calmly (not in an accusing or defensive way), and keeping the discussion to the issue at hand (staying impersonal). When you are the party at fault, an apology and an effort to make things right (a discount, a free dinner, etc.) will go a long way to appeasing an unhappy business associate. If you are the injured party, clearly lay out the problem you are having and offer a reasonable solution.

If you do not think that talking with the other person will work, send a polite letter stating your position (without threatening a lawsuit), which may give the other person some time to respond calmly and reasonably. Most disagreements are resolved with thoughtful communication. If a disagreement becomes a legal dispute—one party threatens or files suit against another, there are a few ways to resolve it:

- **Negotiate a settlement.** This is by far the best and usually the least expensive way to resolve a dispute. There is still time to sit down and work out the dispute amicably. A negotiated settlement is usually preferable, especially in a small community and if you are new to the area. Word travels fast, and you don't want to appear unreasonable or litigious to future customers or fellow business owners.

- **Mediation.** If both parties are in disagreement, and a settlement looks unlikely, you may want to invite a mediator to hear the dispute and offer a resolution. Local business groups can usually recommend a trained mediator. Mediation is not binding, but sometimes the opinion of a neutral third party will be all that is needed to put a conflict to rest.

- **Arbitration.** A final way to settle a disagreement without going to court is through arbitration. Essentially, the arbitrator acts as a private judge, the parties present their cases, and the arbitrator's decision is binding. While somewhat like a court trial, there is less formality and expense and a conflict can be resolved faster than in court.

- **Go to court.** If other means of resolving a dispute have failed or are not likely to occur, you can then take the issue to court. If the amount of money in dispute is small enough to go to small claims court, you can (and will probably be required to) represent yourself. In larger cases, you're likely better off hiring a lawyer, which is always costly.

Keep in mind that just about every business action has possible legal consequences (much like actions in your personal life), but that's no reason to not pursue a dream. Mistakes are made and problems arise, but the best way to deal with them is to address the problem right away, gather as much information as you can about it, and proceed deliberately and fairly in your response.

Hiring Professional Help

In this chapter, we have given a very basic overview of some of the legal and tax considerations a small business may face. With enough time and research, many tasks can be handled on your own. However, there are times when you may need some support, and hiring an attorney to review documentation or a CPA to address tax and bookkeeping issues makes good sense. Generally, the higher the stakes or the more complicated the matter, the more likely you should get some help.

For instance, being sued, buying a business, and starting a lengthy application process (such as for a license to produce alcohol), are situations when hiring professional legal help is the right thing to do. When hiring a professional, look for someone who has experience in the area you need—for instance, if your employee has sued you for discrimination, has the lawyer represented employers in discrimination cases? You will likely find the best person for the job through referrals from people you already trust—if you need help, ask other business owners for their recommendations.

Being able to call on competent professional help can help manage the legal risks associated with your business. The next chapter will take a look at some of the other risks your business might face, and how you can incorporate your business plan into your overall financial and life plans. ●

A Life Plan, a Financial Plan, and a Small Business in Paradise

Many people are halted in their plan to start a small business in paradise by the sense that it would be too risky or seem irresponsible. However, choosing to start and own a small business can be part of a responsible overall financial plan, one that builds wealth and improves your lifestyle. This chapter addresses how to integrate your small business into your overall financial plan, how to manage risk and debt, the importance of separating your personal finances from your business finances, and how to integrate your business into your retirement and estate plans.

Your Piece of the Pie

A small business should serve several purposes within your overall financial plan, as well as your overall life plan. The primary reason most people start small businesses in the first place—whether it's in paradise or elsewhere—is the freedom that comes with being one's own boss. While this independence can come at the price of increased responsibilities and higher risk, many take on the challenge, hoping that happiness will come with the freedom.

"I read somewhere that true happiness is when you own your own business, are involved with the arts, live near the ocean, and have a garden," says Ren Brown, the gallery owner profiled in Chapter 4. "By that definition, I must have found happiness."

If started and managed well, however, a small business can—and should—also help build personal wealth and leave you with more disposable income. From Microsoft founder Bill Gates and Berkshire Hathaway owner Warren Buffett, on down to the owner of the burger franchise around the corner or the plumbing contractor who fixed your sink, successful business owners have all realized something many of us have not—that working for someone else is not necessarily the best way to build wealth.

Consider that, since the 1970s, the average wage of the American worker has actually declined in real terms—in other words, wage increases have not kept up with inflation. During those same years, however, stock market returns have averaged about 11% a year, fueled by soaring corporate profits. As a result, corporate profits—as a percentage of national income—have grown over the past 35 years, while employee compensation has declined, according to the U.S. Labor Department. In other words, it's better to "be the man" than to "work for the man."

To be sure, there are other ways to take part in the growth of corporate profits—many companies offer employee ownership plans, for example. Even owning stocks or mutual funds gives you a small share of that corporate pie. However, all of those means of corporate ownership come with a distinct lack of control over anything the company does—including how it distributes its profits. Additionally, however you hold stock ownership, you can be sure that there will be several financial intermediaries involved, all taking their fees. By the time transaction fees, management fees, front-end loads, back-end loads, and other sales charges are deducted from the purchase, sale, or management of your stock ownership, your return may be well below the 11% annual return you anticipate from the stock market.

Owning your own business is another way of participating in the growth of corporate America, allowing you to build your own wealth while exercising more control over your investment. While you do not have power over all of the factors affecting your business, your planning and efforts will be the primary components of your success or failure. When you add living in paradise—and possibly happiness—into the equation, the overall returns look even better. The extraordinary appeal of owning a small business in paradise is being able to experience the lifestyle you want while working toward your dream, and when you have built your business, being able to look back and say, "Yes, it was all really worth it."

Your Financial Plan

Recognizing the potential benefits and gains of owning your own business doesn't mean you should stop investing in the stock market. That's where a good financial plan becomes important. Part of that plan should include a decision as to how much you want to invest in yourself (in the form of your business), and how much you want to invest in others (in the form of stocks, bonds, mutual funds, etc.).

One of the first things a financial advisor will likely warn you against is viewing any investment in a vacuum. You may own stock in a great company, or a top-performing mutual fund, or a hot new exchange-traded fund, but your portfolio may nevertheless fail if you do not keep an eye on the big picture— namely, how all your investments work together. A solid financial plan assures that your overall portfolio combines securities with varied levels of risk and expected returns to match your own investment goals and risk tolerance. For example, equity investments may provide long-term gains, while bonds may temper equity's price volatility with a safe and secure stream of income, with cash investments offering additional peace of mind and quick accessibility for rainy day situations. Global investments and, if your portfolio is large enough, alternative investments such as hedge funds and private equity, can provide diversity and shield against swings in the national economy and stock market. A good financial planner will consider and integrate into your financial plan not only your securities investment portfolio, but your real estate holdings, insurance, and other personal assets.

What financial planners might not tell you—and they should!—is that your small business should be considered as part of that overall financial plan. Your business is an investment with its own level of risk, an asset with its own potential liabilities, and operates as just one component of your financial picture. If you are considering starting a small business in paradise, there are two ways to try to reduce the risk of your venture—managing the risk in your overall financial plan (of which your business would be a part) and minimizing the risk of problems in your business.

Managing Risk in Your Overall Financial Plan

A good financial plan takes into consideration how all of your assets, such as an investment portfolio of stocks, bonds, and other equities, real estate, and any businesses you own, work together to support you and your family in the best way possible. Additionally, that plan should be structured to keep your overall financial risk at a manageable level, much the same way that a well-considered investment portfolio would. In any investment portfolio, there are different types of risk to consider. For example, any asset within your portfolio has its own set of risks which affect the returns of that asset—a delay in the delivery of the next operating system could affect the price of your stock in Microsoft, or a new pharmaceutical bill that passes Congress could affect the price of your stock in Johnson & Johnson. And then there are portfolio risks that affect the returns of your overall investment portfolio—if your portfolio is heavily weighted toward one sector of the stock market or another, that will add to your overall portfolio risk, while if you have assets that are not correlated to one another (their prices don't move in tandem), that will lower your overall portfolio risk. Each asset in your portfolio plays a part in that overall portfolio risk.

Likewise, as a small business owner, your business will likely play a substantial role in your overall financial plan. Similar to specific risks of a particular stock affecting your investment portfolio (and consequently, your overall financial picture), risks specifically related to your business could affect the business's revenue stream and profit, and consequently, your overall financial plan. For example, risks for a small business in paradise might include a lighter-than-expected snowfall, a hurricane, a change in consumer tastes, a fire in your warehouse, a new competitor across the street, or a deterioration in your own health and ability to continue managing the business.

Managing risk to your overall financial plan includes balancing those business risks with the risks of the different components of the plan. It's important to find a good financial planner or investment advisor who will understand the role your business plays in your financial picture—as well as the particular risks that may affect your business—and can help you manage both the business-specific and overall financial plan risks. If you don't already have someone capable who you trust, start by looking for a fee-based investment advisor, known in the industry as a registered investment advisor (RIA), as opposed to someone who works for commissions on the sales of securities he or she makes. RIAs are more likely to serve your interest because their income comes from you, instead of from the investment companies whose products they sell. Whoever advises you, make sure to ask as many questions as you need to ensure that an advisor isn't encouraging you to increase your investment in stocks or bonds simply because that is where he or she makes money, or because he or she has no understanding of your small business. Don't feel you have to work with the first person you meet—it may take some time to find someone who is interested in your business as well as your investment portfolio.

A good financial planner or wealth manager will take the risk element that your new business is introducing into your life and integrate that with the rest of your personal financial plan. He or she should be able to offer a variety of suggestions depending on your situation. If your business will inject a high amount of risk into your financial plan, for example, a planner may suggest how to reduce the risk level in another component of your financial plan, such as in your investment portfolio. If you are concerned about loss of income while building the business, he or she may advise cutting down the growth portion of your investment portfolio and beefing up the income portion, with the dual goals of reducing your overall portfolio volatility and generating more income for your family to live on during the start-up period. A financial planner may point out that risks common to your type of business may also affect particular assets in your investment portfolio, so suggest changing the mix of your investment portfolio to help diversify your holdings and reduce your overall risk. Additionally, he or she may believe you have too much invested in one asset (your business, your investment portfolio, your home, etc.), thereby endangering your chances for building wealth, retiring comfortably, and leaving something tangible for your heirs, and recommend a rebalancing of your assets. Among many other possible recommendations, a financial planner may also suggest increasing your insurance coverage or transferring assets into a trust for your family.

Working With Financial Planners

If you meet with a financial planner, make sure to prepare for your meeting by creating at least a rough monthly budget—list your sources of income, such as rental income from an investment property, a second job, other investment or family income, and income you can expect from the business (you may not expect any at first), and your monthly expenses. The planner will also need to see a list of your assets and debts. Take a copy of your business plan, if you have not yet started your business, or recent financials if you have begun business operations.

Managing Specific Business Risks

Besides managing the risk of your overall financial plan, the other way to reduce the potential perils of starting a business in paradise is to address risks inherent in running the business itself.

Know Your Limit

Deciding how much you will invest in your business before starting will help prevent you from draining other—or all of—your assets into your business. Start-up costs can sometimes get out of hand, your business is likely to experience some bad times as well as good, and there may be occasions when you'll be tempted to use your personal rainy day money to pay the business's operating expenses. Drawing a clear line between your personal and business finances will help reduce the risk of your venture to you and your family.

"You certainly wouldn't invest your kids' educations or your retirement funds in a bar in the Caribbean," says Keith Savitz, an entrepreneur profiled in Chapter 5. Savitz says he's always looked at his investment in a restaurant-bar in St. Thomas as "risk capital" within his overall financial plan. "In other words, don't go into it unless you'd be all right if you lost your entire investment."

While stories abound about entrepreneurs putting their last few dollars into a business before finally reaching success, going to the financial brink is a sure way to drive yourself to distraction and disrupt your family, if you have one. Before investing in your paradise venture, make sure your family has enough readily accessible funds, such as cash and cash equivalents (certificates of deposit and money-market funds), for a comfortable period of time. While that length of time depends on your own risk tolerance, it should be at least as long as you believe it will take for your business, in combination with other sources of income, to support you.

That's not to say you should never use your own capital to start a business. Most successful businesses are begun with the owner providing part, if not all, of the start-up capital. Just make sure you know where to draw the line—don't commit more of your personal finances than you can afford to lose. In Chapter 6, one of the items on the ten-step plan to get started is determining how you will finance your business. That plan should clearly delineate which of your assets are acceptable sources for business financing, and which are not.

Managing Debt

At one time or another, many of us have done the credit card juggling act—transferring a balance from a higher-rate card to a new card with a low promotional interest rate. Of course, the problem with this strategy is twofold: first, that low promotional rate will change to a much higher rate down the road, and if the debt is not paid off in time, the card holder is stuck with paying that rate; and second, even at the higher rate, some may not stop using the card if there is credit still available. Clearly, successfully juggling credit cards takes discipline.

Running a small business requires the same discipline. Many new business owners take on some form of debt to get started, but taking on debt without a solid plan for repaying it increases your business risk significantly. Just like determining how much of your resources will be devoted to the business, know how much debt you are willing to assume. Many financing sources require you—as the small business owner—to guarantee the repayment of the loan. This includes credit cards and bank loans, so before taking on that debt, make sure that you can afford the interest, and can pay back what you borrow.

As you research your dream business, include in your questions to answer what level of debt is considered acceptable for your business. You might find this answer online, in a class about your business, from your investment advisor, or from others in the business community.

Your Local Banker

If you are planning on doing business in a small community, consider doing your banking with a locally owned and respected bank. Bank executives will likely be more accessible to you, are usually interested in your success (and the community's prosperity), and may be willing to talk over various business decisions, especially those regarding debt. While they will likely offer a conservative view, they can provide a good counterbalance to the pressure you may sometimes feel to borrow more money.

There are multiple sources of credit, as described in "Consider Your Financing" in Chapter 6. (See also *Legal Guide for Starting & Running a Small Business,* by Fred Steingold (Nolo), for a more in-depth discussion of different types of financing.) While there are many types to choose from, you can help manage your risk if you watch out for the easy capital sources. You know what they are—credit cards and retirement funds. For instance, it might make sense in a pinch to use credit card debt to help start a business—according to media reports, many successful businesses were started that way. But do not rely on credit cards for any significant long-term debt—the interest rates are punishing compared to other debt resources. If your goal is to reduce the risk of your small business in paradise, limit your credit card use to charges you can pay off every month. (For convenience, you may want to have a credit card in the business's name, as it may offer a lower rate of interest than personal cards. A separate card will also make it easier to track business expenses.)

Exercise similar caution if you are considering borrowing start-up capital from the retirement savings plan you may have established at work (assuming your 401(k) plan allows business loans). In your excitement and optimism about a new business, it may be tempting to tap these funds, but not if you are trying to minimize your personal or family risk. While a loan from your 401(k) may offer a lower interest rate than some other sources of financing, withdrawing those funds eats away at the returns from your retirement plan. That is because a 401(k) loan is funded by selling off investments within your account—the fewer the assets, the lower the return. Additionally, once you start drawing on those funds, it becomes easier to continue to do so (although the retirement plan may have limits on the percentage you can borrow). Remember that loans from your 401(k) usually must be repaid within a fairly short period of time—a few years—depending on your plan.

Insurance

Purchasing the appropriate types of insurance and the right amount of coverage is another way to reduce overall risk for both you and your business, and is part of any prudent financial plan. What kind of insurance coverage—both for you and your business—and how much, will depend on the likelihood of an insured event occurring and your own risk tolerance. In some cases, a particular type of insurance will be required by law or by third parties, such as lenders to your business. Working with your financial planner and an insurance broker with a good reputation in the community is the place to start in determining what you will need. Beyond that, each policy should be analyzed based on the risk reduction and peace of mind it brings to you and your business, versus the cost of the insurance.

With respect to types of business insurance, you'll likely need liability insurance to protect you if someone entering your business is injured. Some general liability insurance policies may also provide other protections, such as insuring against copyright or trademark claims. Additionally, if there is a chance that any of the products you make or sell could harm someone, you should consider product liability coverage. If you have employees, you will be obligated by law to carry workers' compensation insurance, which covers your liability for employees' injuries on the job.

Property insurance is essential to any small business owner who owns his or her facility or has inventory or expensive equipment. Additionally, living in paradise can pose natural risks less likely to occur in the city. Therefore, in addition to standard property coverage, make sure your policy—or a separate one—insures the building and its contents against natural disasters occurring in your region, such as floods, hurricanes, forest fires, and so on. Your property insurance should also cover you against theft, and any damages your business might cause to other tenants of the building. If you lease, you'll want to purchase tenant's insurance that covers anything the owners' policies do not.

Another type of insurance you may want to consider is typically referred to as "business interruption" insurance, which is intended to cover your business's lost income if your business is shut down by a disaster. Business interruption insurance should also cover expenses for keeping your business going while waiting for its facility to be restored. If your property is unique, and it would cost you dearly to have the business shut down, business interruption insurance is a good way to reduce your risk.

While you are covering the business risks, do not forget to take care of yourself. If you are considering leaving a job, you may also be leaving the comfort of severance packages, health benefits, workers' compensation, and other employee benefits. The loss of all of these should be considered as risks in starting your own business. At a minimum, consider extending the health package of your former employer under the COBRA program. Although you will be responsible for the premiums each month, the coverage is likely more comprehensive and less expensive than any personal health insurance policies you can get on your own. Since your right to COBRA coverage extends for 18 months (some states extend this time period), you will have time to get your business up and running—and, if your business has employees or more than one owner, it will likely be able to get its own health insurance policy.

Retirement Planning

If you're successful in managing business debt and risk, your business may become an integral component of your personal wealth. In addition to generating income that can then be reinvested, a business is itself an investment. With good management, its value can grow over time, and that increased value opens up other opportunities for increasing your wealth. For instance, a more valuable business may serve as collateral for loans or credit lines to start other businesses or purchase property, all with their own capacity for appreciation. Accessible funds can also be used to pay for your family's emergency needs or medical expenses. In that sense, wealth building brings peace of mind and can be a valuable substitute for the job security you worry about leaving behind with a nine-to-five job. As a substantial factor in your personal wealth, a small business in paradise should also be an important part of your retirement planning.

Establishing a possible exit plan even before starting your business is key to these tasks. Ask yourself what you see happening with the business in the future—when it comes time for you to retire from the business, will it simply cease to exist? Do you plan on selling it? Will you allow your employees or partners to take over ownership? Will you pass it on to your heirs?

Making these decisions early in the life of the business will make it more likely to achieve your desired outcome. For instance, not all businesses can be easily bought and sold. If, for example, you own a small marketing agency whose projects are mostly one-time gigs, with no long-term contracts, you have a slim chance of selling that company for a reasonable sum. In general, if you own any business that depends almost entirely on your skills or personality, chances are it won't be able to continue without you, and any potential buyer will recognize that. If you focus your efforts not just on boosting your company's income, but on boosting its value, chances are greater that you'll have something valuable to sell when the time comes.

Building value can be achieved in various ways, one of which is developing a variety of income sources—perhaps your marketing agency not only develops marketing plans, but also can be hired to do event planning or develops an expertise in designing product packaging for a particular industry (wine labels, for instance). Diversification of revenue streams will make your business unique and hence more valuable. Establishing long-term client relationships also adds value, and of course, tangible assets such as buildings, equipment, and inventory all add to the potential sale price for your business. Finally, hiring and training the right team may make your business look more appealing to a potential buyer when it's time for you to leave, or better yet, key employees may be the ones who will buy your business from you (which offers an additional incentive for them to stay).

That value can then be leveraged to help build your retirement nest egg. If, for example, you build the business successfully to the point where it has a strong sale value, it might make sense to sell all or part of it. The income from that sale can then be reinvested to supplement your retirement income. Or, you could structure the sale so that you retain an equity stake for yourself and share in distributions to owners, which amounts can also be used to supplement your retirement income.

Of course, your financial planner can help you estimate how much your future business income can contribute to your retirement, and your retirement savings plan can take that into account. In addition to any remaining retirement funds you have from previous jobs, you'll probably want to continue investing in tax-advantaged retirement accounts during the time you own and operate your business. In addition to 401(k) plans, there are various types of retirement accounts and plans appropriate for sole proprietors and businesses with very few employees, including a SEP-IRA, a simple IRA, or an individual 401(k). See *The Retirement Bible,* by Lynn O'Shaughnessy (Wiley), for more about small business retirement plans.

Boost Your Chance at Happiness

While there are plenty of happy and successful business owners out there, there are also a number of successful entrepreneurs (especially in big cities) who, in spite of their success—or perhaps because of it—just aren't happy people. While paradise is often the cure for that, even in paradise you may find small business owners who are stressed, overworked, and tired. More often than not, those are the people who haven't been able to match business success with a pleasing personal financial picture and a comfortable retirement. Your business, your financial plan, your debt, and your retirement plan should all work seamlessly together toward the ultimate goal of a healthy and happy lifestyle. Managing your business risk and that of your overall financial plan can contribute greatly to accomplishing that goal. ●

All Hail Jimmy Buffett

Back in Chapter 1 were listed some of the reasons that people choose to start small businesses in paradise. Maybe they're sick of the corporate rat race, deriving less and less satisfaction from their jobs. Or maybe it's city life itself that they're tired of—the traffic, the pollution, the noise, and the stress of the concrete jungle. Maybe they desire a chance to put their passion to work, or perhaps they hear the call of the wild, and feel the urge to get back to nature.

Whatever it is, choosing to start a small business in paradise usually begins as a lifestyle decision. Or, for those who are familiar with his music, it's the chance to live a Jimmy Buffet song! From "Margaritaville" to "Changes in Latitude," Buffett's songs are all about the life that many want to lead, but for whatever reason—financial pressures, personal obligations, or simply not feeling ready—haven't yet pursued. In fact, Jimmy Buffett does a good job of describing what many would-be-paradise-entrepreneurs feel in his book, *A Pirate Looks at Fifty*. For Buffett, turning 50 "can be a ball of snakes that conjures up immediate thoughts of mortality and accountability. ('What have I done with my life?') Or, it can be a great excuse to reward yourself for just getting there." Of course, this self-questioning can begin at any age and be triggered by any milestone. To many, the reward for managing life so far is moving to paradise and opening their own businesses.

Whether it's a bed and breakfast, a bar, a surf shop, or a winery, the desire to open a small business in paradise inevitably has something to do with restoring balance in our lives. Some people, like Bob the Surfer and Keoki Flagg, knew exactly what they wanted at an early age and moved to paradise to pursue it. Many of us start off adulthood in a different way—capturing corporate jobs, starting families, and managing a myriad of responsibilities. These achievements should be recognized and celebrated. Somewhere between our childhood and our current place in the world, however, we may feel that we have lost something—something important!—and we want to get it back, or at least try. We need to restore balance between life and career, and go back to living, instead of just surviving.

This is not to suggest that starting a business is a piece of cake. Buffett's songs also offer the bittersweet notion that paradise isn't all about, as he puts it, "boats, beaches, bars, and ballads." Indeed, seeking paradise does exact a cost. Starting any small business brings the challenges of hard work, raising capital (or spending your own), learning new things, and moving from the known to the unknown.

One thing's for sure though—not a single one of the small business owners interviewed for this book regretted their decision to move to paradise and start their own business. In fact, for many of them it was the best decision they ever made, and their only regret was not doing it sooner. Even those who started a business and are now considering leaving it seem to feel a sense of fulfillment, happy they took the chance and satisfied their curiosity.

Some of you now finishing this book might feel deterred from your dream by the realization that opening a small business in paradise isn't so simple and may not always be, well, paradise. Others—hopefully, most of you—feel encouraged by learning how to go about it, and hearing the stories and practical advice of those who have followed their desire. If you are one of those people and decide to start making your way to paradise, visit www.smallbizinparadise.com and join the discussion board. Swapping stories about your business, your experience, and your community is one of the best ways to avoid repeating costly mistakes others have already made, and to find creative solutions to the typical paradise problems discussed throughout this book. Good luck, and bon voyage! ●

Index

C

I

J

K

W

Z

Get the Latest in the Law

Nolo's Legal Updater
We'll send you an email whenever a new edition of your book is published! Sign up at **www.nolo.com/legalupdater**.

Updates at Nolo.com
Check **www.nolo.com/update** to find recent changes in the law that affect the current edition of your book.

Nolo Customer Service
To make sure that this edition of the book is the most recent one, call us at **800-728-3555** and ask one of our friendly customer service representatives (7:00 am to 6:00 pm PST, weekdays only). Or find out at **www.nolo.com**.

Complete the Registration & Comment Card ...
... and we'll do the work for you! Just indicate your preferences below:

Registration & Comment Card

NAME   DATE

ADDRESS

CITY   STATE   ZIP

PHONE   EMAIL

COMMENTS

WAS THIS BOOK EASY TO USE?   (VERY EASY)   5   4   3   2   1   (VERY DIFFICULT)

☐ Yes, you can quote me in future Nolo promotional materials. *Please include phone number above.*

☐ Yes, send me **Nolo's Legal Updater** via email when a new edition of this book is available.

Yes, I want to sign up for the following email newsletters:

    ☐ **NoloBriefs** (monthly)
    ☐ **Nolo's Special Offer** (monthly)
    ☐ **Nolo's BizBriefs** (monthly)
    ☐ **Every Landlord's Quarterly** (four times a year)

☐ Yes, you can give my contact info to carefully selected partners whose products may be of interest to me.

SPAR1

NOLO

Nolo
950 Parker Street
Berkeley, CA 94710-9867
www.nolo.com

YOUR LEGAL COMPANION